The cocoa and chocolate museum

When we first became interested in the histor
chocolate, this most noble and delicious of foo
we were far from thinking that its main ingredien ...oa,
had such a passionate and glorious past and that so many nations continue to consume and venerate it, as their ancestors did thousands of years ago.

Moreover, we would never have believed that we would find such a warm welcome and kindheartedness in the peasant farmers who live very simple lives, sometimes in the most precarious conditions.
We hope that our museums and the actions we are taking through our Cocoa Development Fund will help to promote the image and the consumption of chocolate and will enable the cocoa farmers, their workers and their families to improve to a certain extent their living conditions.

We have opened Choco-Story museums in Bruges, Prague and Paris, but they have not all been conceived along the same lines.

This booklet is therefore not intended as a guide to one of our museums in particular, but to give you some general information on the fascinating history of cocoa and chocolate.

We hope you enjoy reading it.

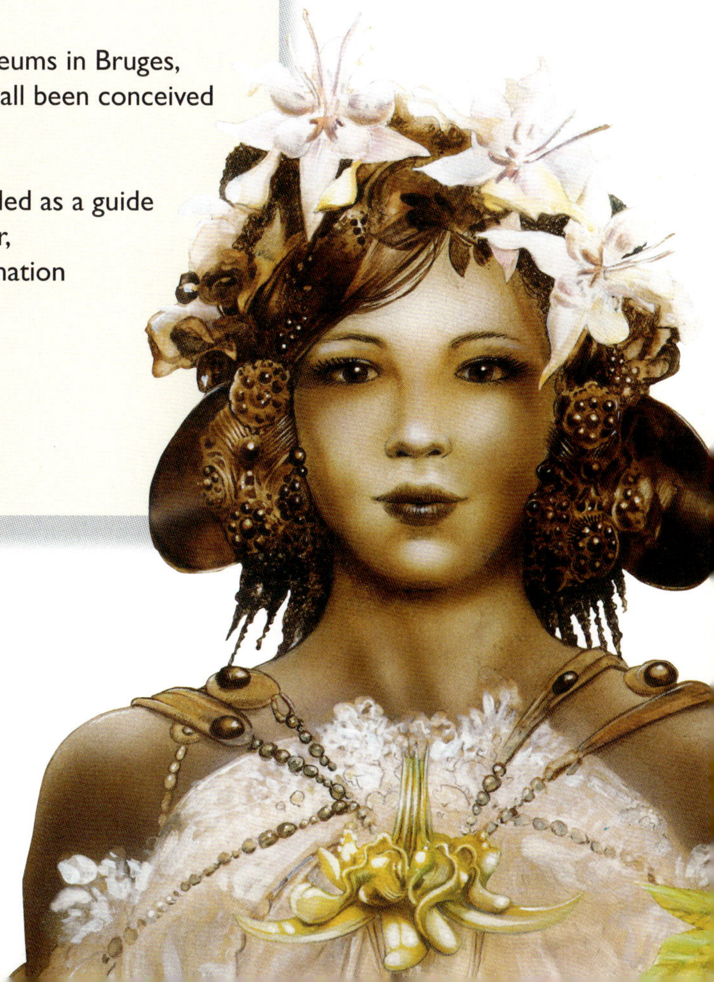

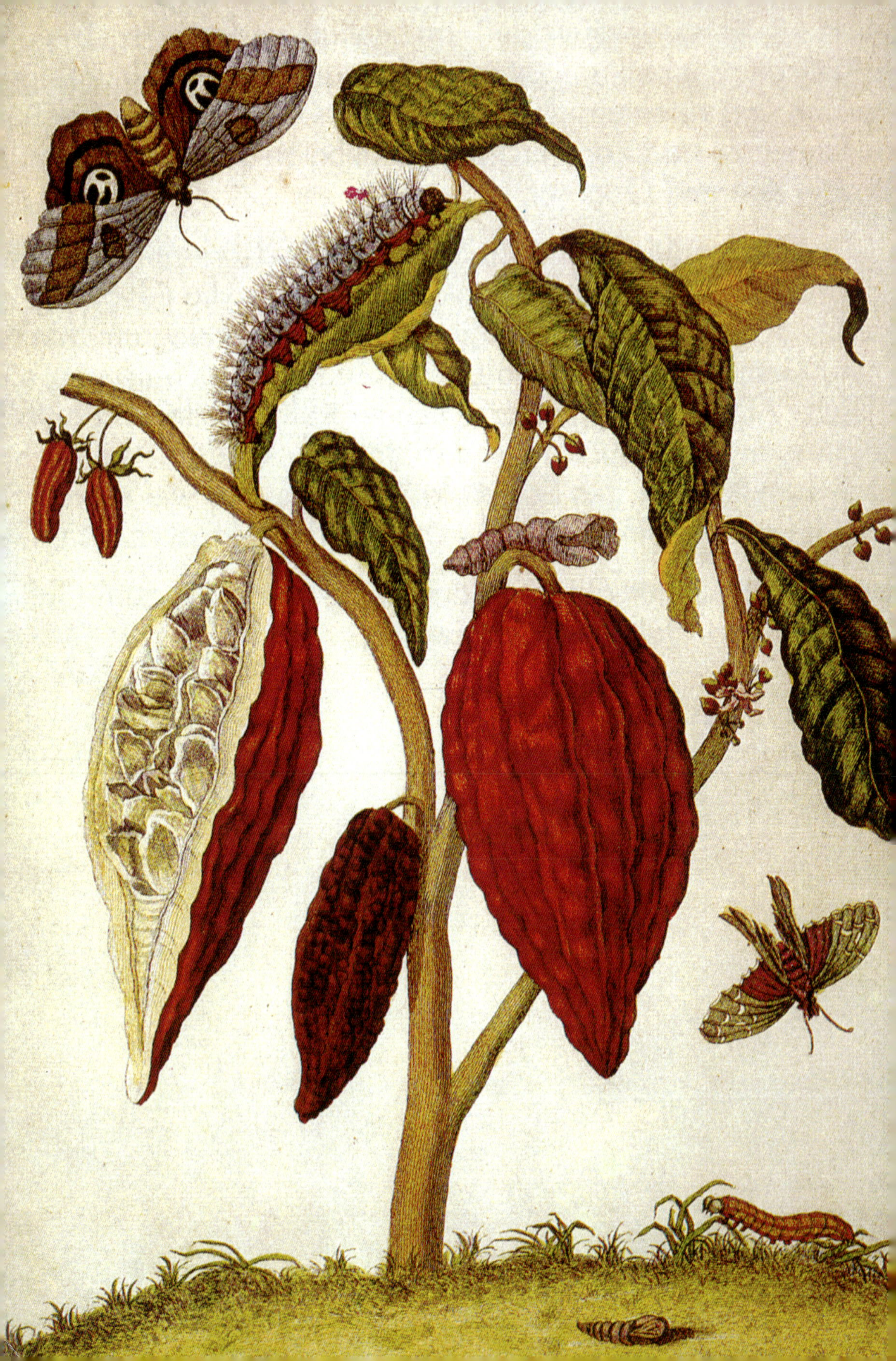

The very long history of cocoa

It all started nearly 4,000 years ago.

Recent research has enabled archaeologists to conclude that in the region of Veracruz in Mexico, the pre-Olmecs used cocoa to make chocolate-flavoured drinks around 2000 BC as did the Mokayas from southern Chiapas, near Soconusco, in about 1850 BC.

At this time, the drink was spicy being made from cocoa and corn to which chilli, Mexican peppers (allspice) and vanilla were added.

It remained spicy until the beginning of the 16th century when Spanish nuns started adding sugar, cloves and cinnamon in order to make the drink sweeter.

It stayed this way until the beginning of the 18th century when solid eating chocolate was produced.

So the use of cocoa goes back 4,000 years, whilst the history of chocolate started just 200 years ago.

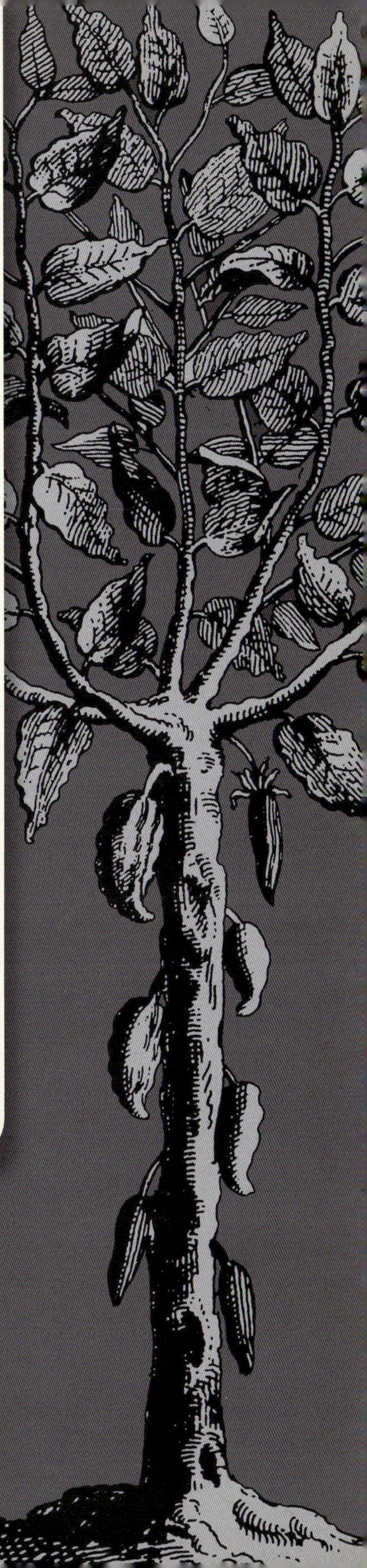

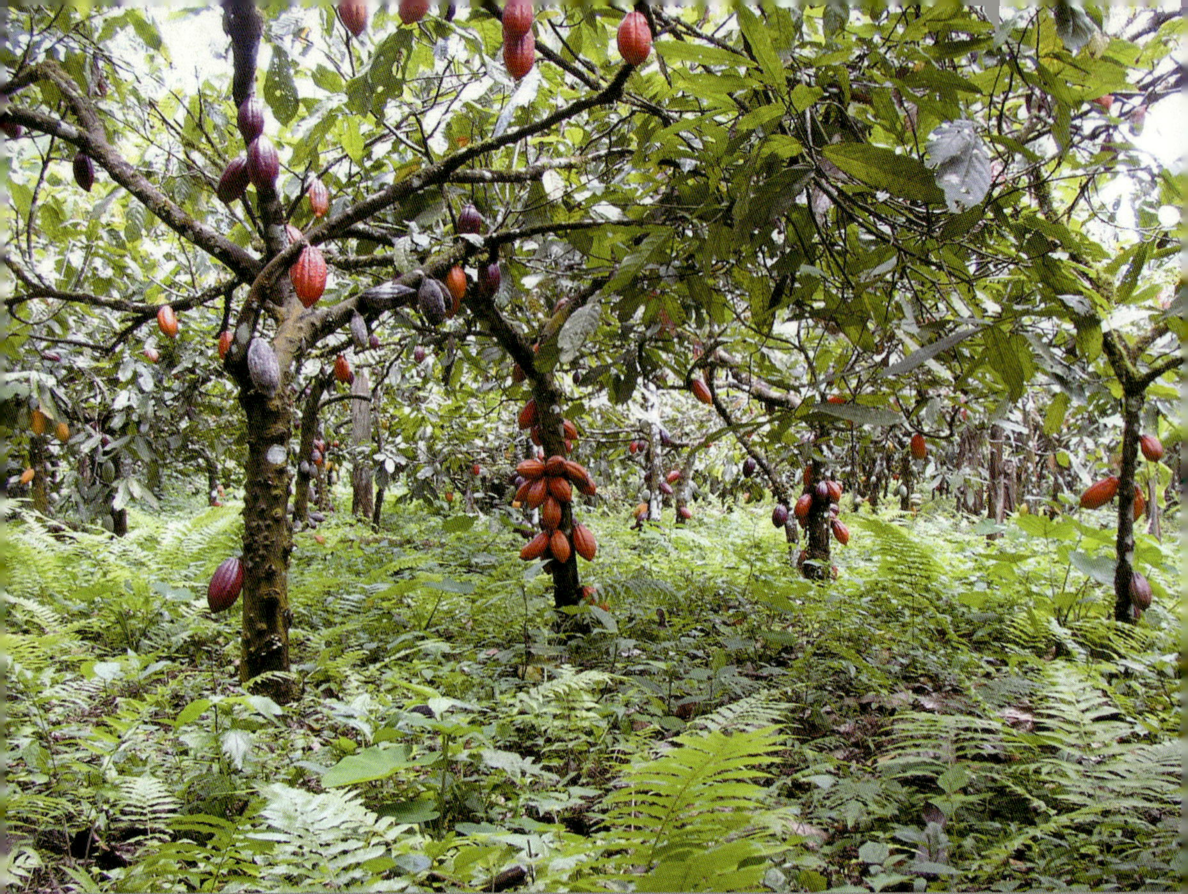

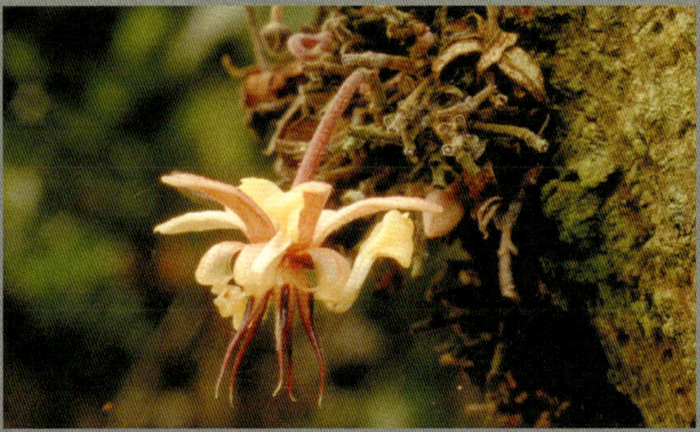

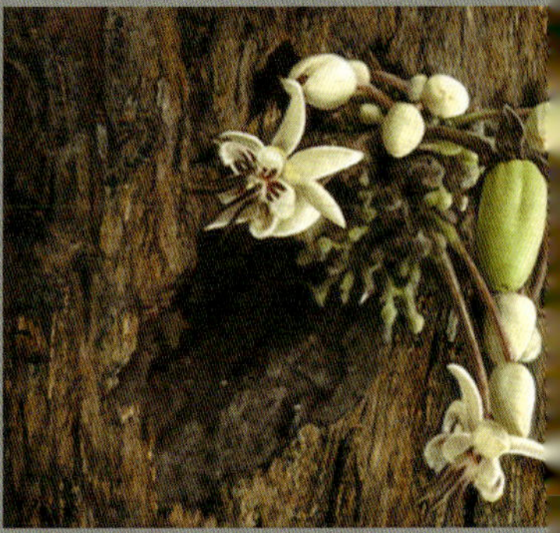

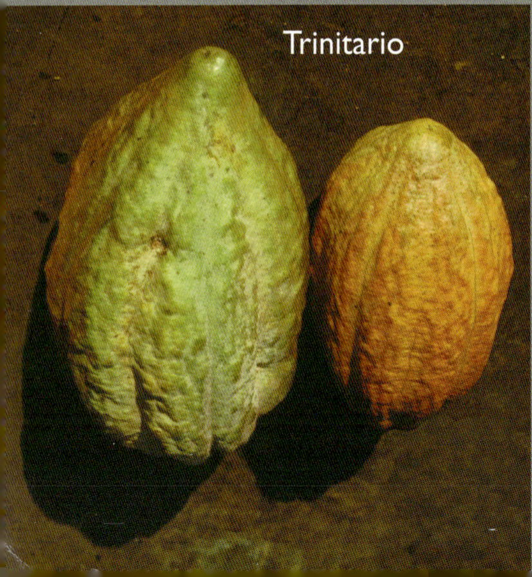
Trinitario

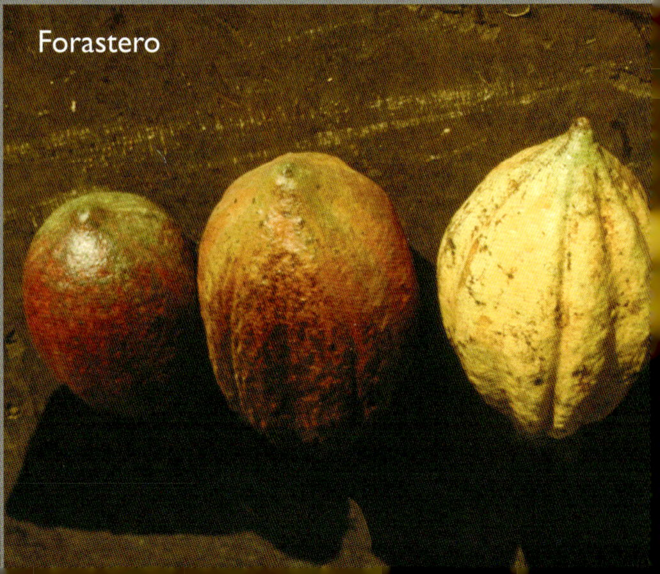
Forastero

The cacao tree

The cacao tree likes heat and humidity but fears the sun and the wind.
It is cultivated between 20 degrees north and south of the equator.

Taller trees, such as banana or other fruit-bearing trees, protect the cacao tree by keeping it in the shade.

If left to its own, the cacao tree can grow as high as 8 to 10 metres, but it is frequently cut back to a height of 3 or 4 metres in order to make harvesting easier.

The cacao tree bears fruit for the first time in its sixth year.

Around about 1,000 flowers grow each year on the trunk and the main branches.
However, only 1 to 3% of the flowers develop into fruit once they have been pollinated by tiny little flies.

Hence, every tree bears between 20 to 40 fruits, called pods. Each pod contains between 20 and 40 cocoa beans.

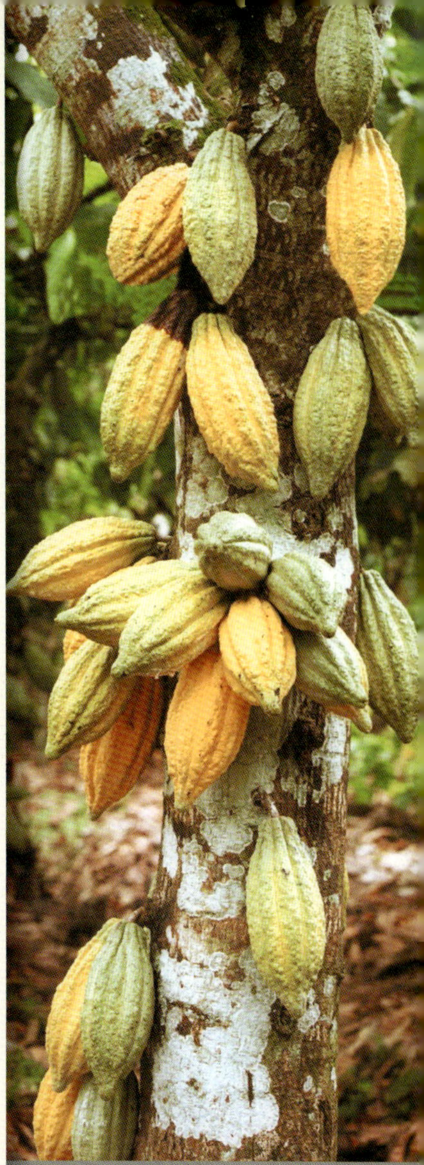

Criollo

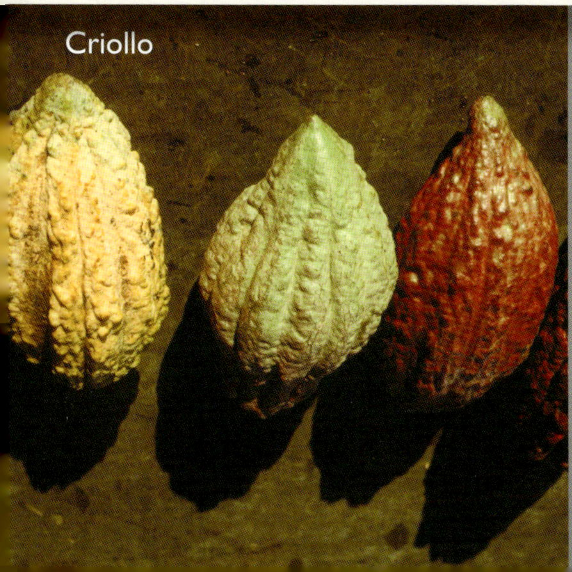

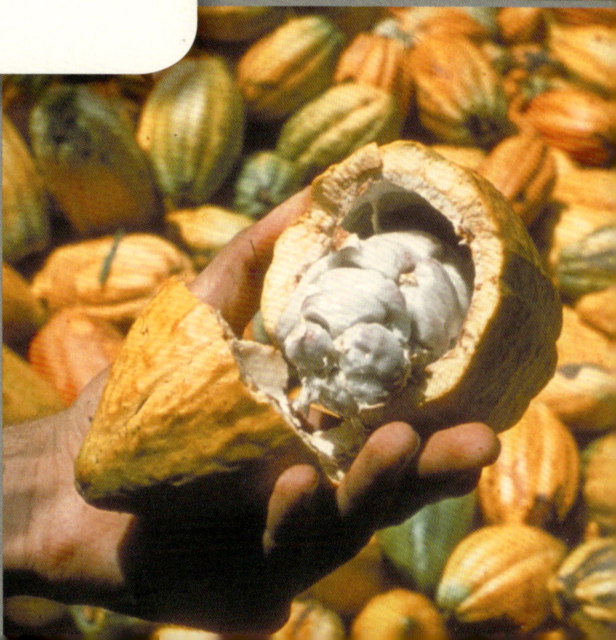

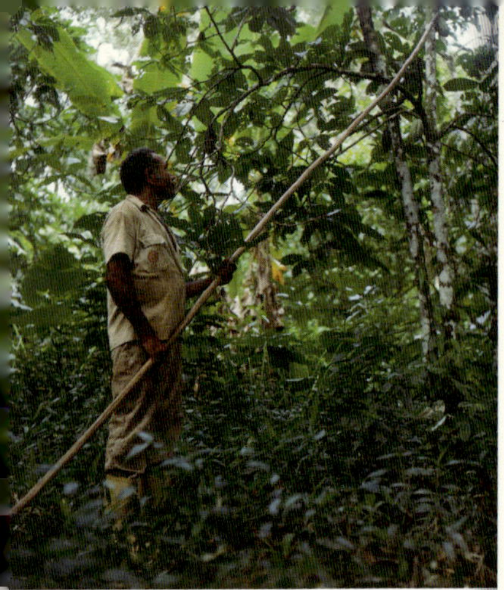

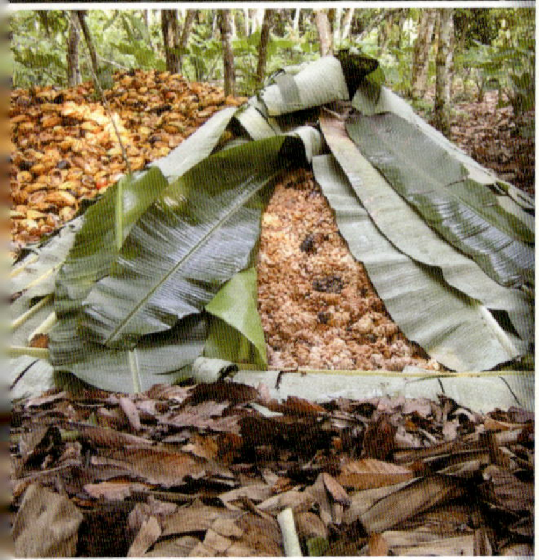

Harvest and fermentation

Harvest takes place twice a year, between April and July and September and December. The cocoa pods are cut down using a knife attached to a long pole.

As soon as they have been harvested, the cocoa pods are sliced in two. The cocoa beans, covered in a layer of pulp, are removed and piled into heaps.

The heaps are covered with banana leaves and left to ferment. Fermentation plays a very important role and is critical in the development of the best flavours and aromas.

Next the cocoa beans are left to dry in the sun in order to reduce the amount of moisture from 60 to 6%, which ensures their conservation.

The dried beans are then packed in hessian sacks.

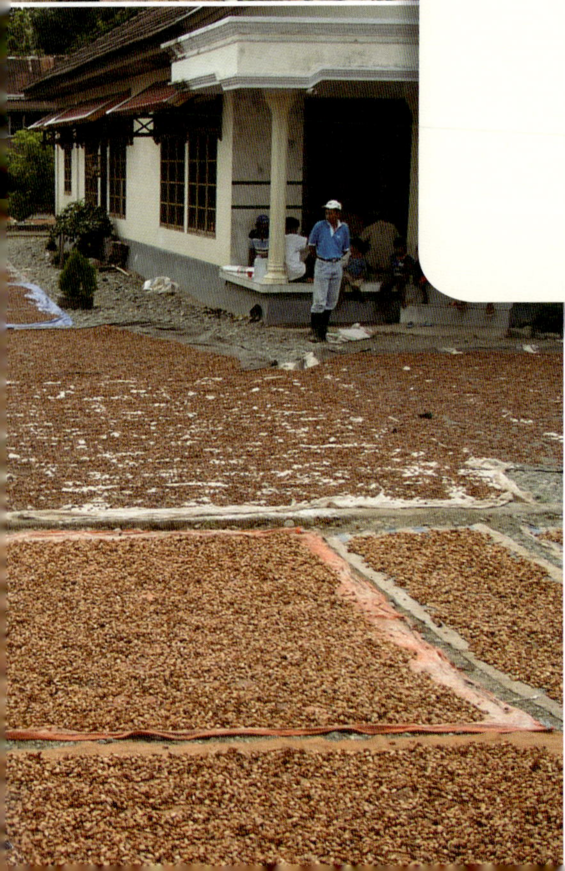

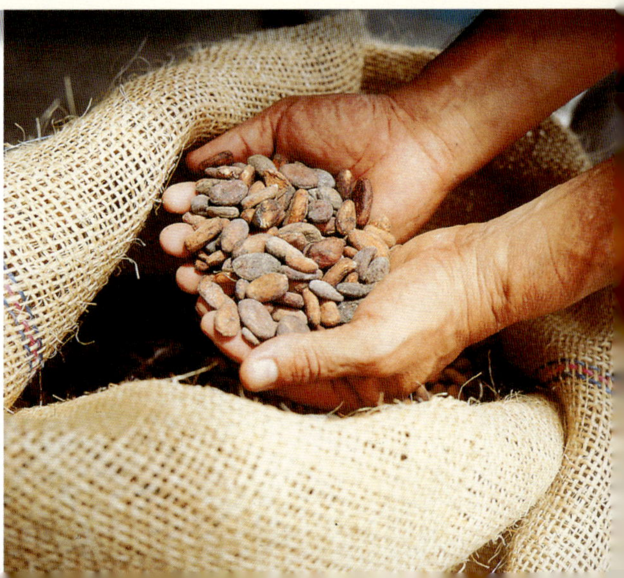

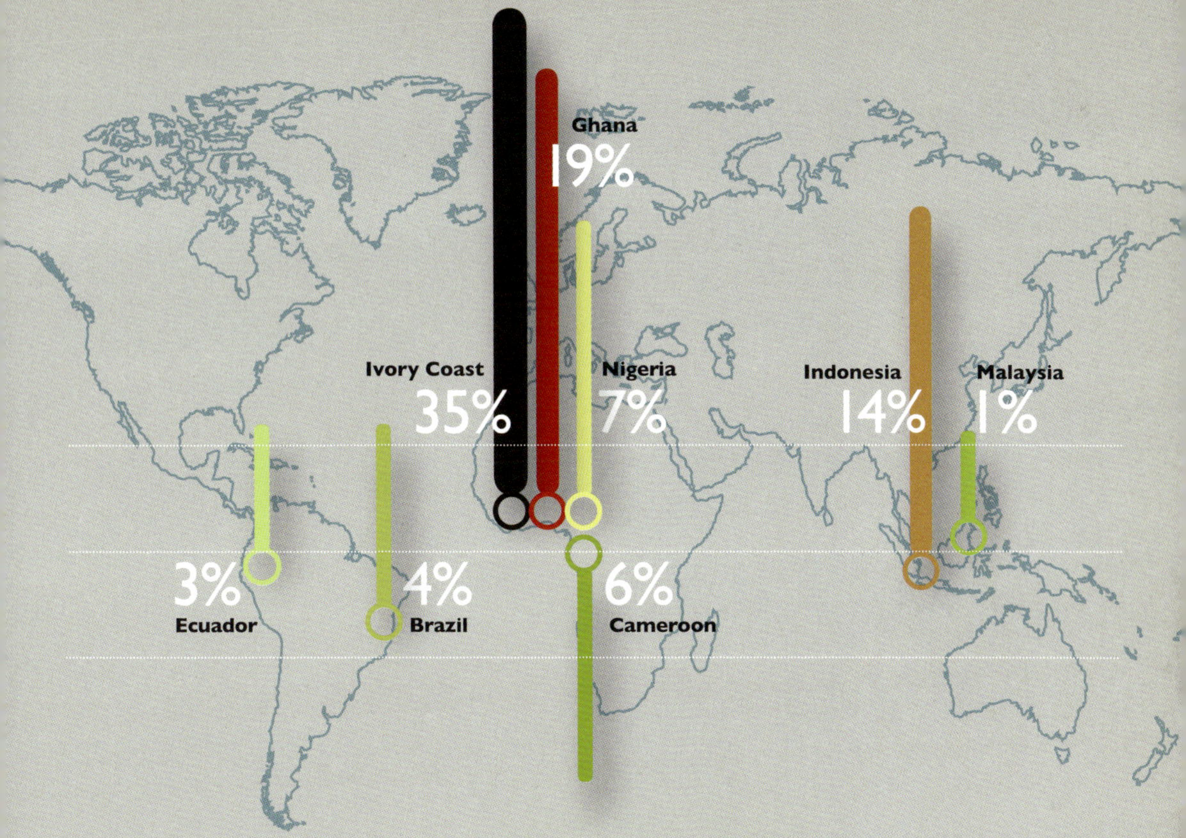

% of cocoa production worldwide		
	35%	Ivory Coast
	19%	Ghana
	14%	Indonesia
	7%	Nigeria
	6%	Cameroon
	4%	Brazil
	3%	Ecuador
	1%	Malaysia
	11%	Others

The cocoa-producing countries

Whilst at the time of the Olmecs and the Mayas Mexico was one of the first countries to grow cocoa, today its annual production only represents 1% of total world production.

The local authorities and cocoa farmers alike are making great efforts in order to fight and eradicate the monilia fungus which has caused production to fall from 30,000 tonnes a year to around just 10,000 tonnes a year.

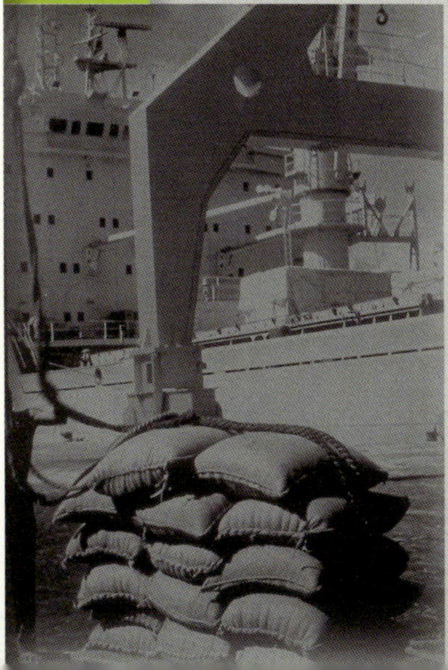

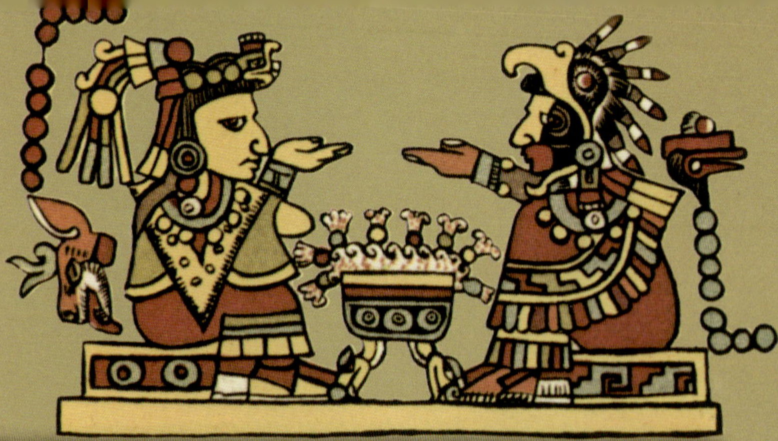

Offerings to the Gods

The ancient people believed that everything that existed on earth was part of one set of beings.

The trees and animals were their brothers.

The mountains and forests, the springs, rivers and caves were all sacred places where the Gods lived.

Worship took place on altars made by 'X-men' or priests according to the particular circumstances and on the platforms of pyramids and in caves on altars made of stone.

They burnt incense called POM in the Maya language, believing that the smoke would hasten their prayers towards the Gods.

As the Gods gave men on earth water to drink and food to eat, it was necessary to thank them in return.

The Indians slit or pierced their tongues or their ear lobes using cactus spikes, skates' tails or flakes of obsidian. They let their blood seep over the cocoa beans or they mixed it with a cocoa-flavoured drink and offered the mixture to the Gods.

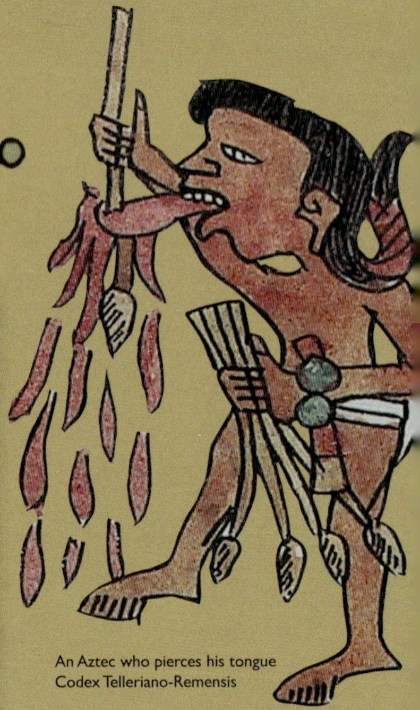

An Aztec who pierces his tongue
Codex Telleriano-Remensis

The Maya's pierce their ears and spill the blood over the beans
Codex Madrid

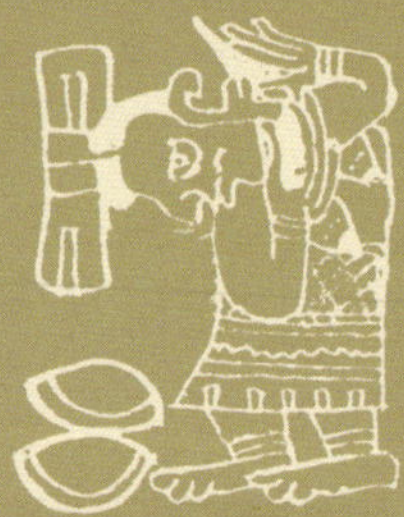

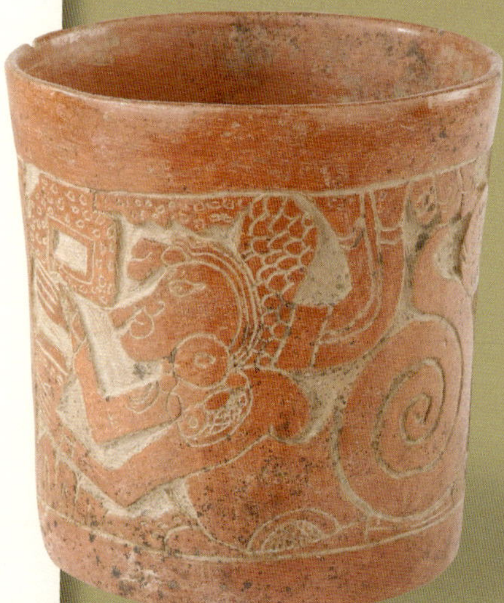

Preparing cocoa-flavoured drinks

The cocoa beans were roasted, winnowed and crushed. The resulting paste was mixed with corn paste. The latter was obtained by cooking the corn with a little quicklime.

This process is called nixtamalization and was used to soften and remove the tough skin covering the corn seeds. Once the cooked corn had been rinsed several times it was ground to a paste.

According to the traditions that prevailed in the different regions, Mexican peppers (allspice), achiote and chillies were added to the mixture of cocoa and corn pastes to make a spicy drink.

The beverage was aerated before being drunk, either by blowing air through a tube placed laterally on the recipient or by pouring the liquid from a certain height from one recipient into another. Later on another method was invented consisting of using a foamer or molinillo that was rubbed energetically between the palms of the hands in order to make it rotate and produce froth.

Kings used to sip the cocoa-flavoured drink from small dishes made of gold. Priests and the nobility drank it from ceramic, carved or painted cups.
Ordinary people seldom had the occasion to taste this drink, but if they did it was from goblets made from the fruit of the jicaro or from gourds.

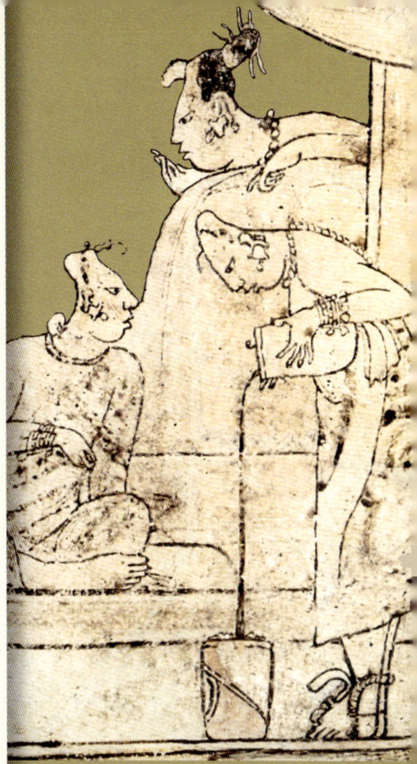

Illustration on a Mayan vase
Princeton Art Museum, © Justin Kerr

Aztec indians use the molinillo to prepare the cocoa drink

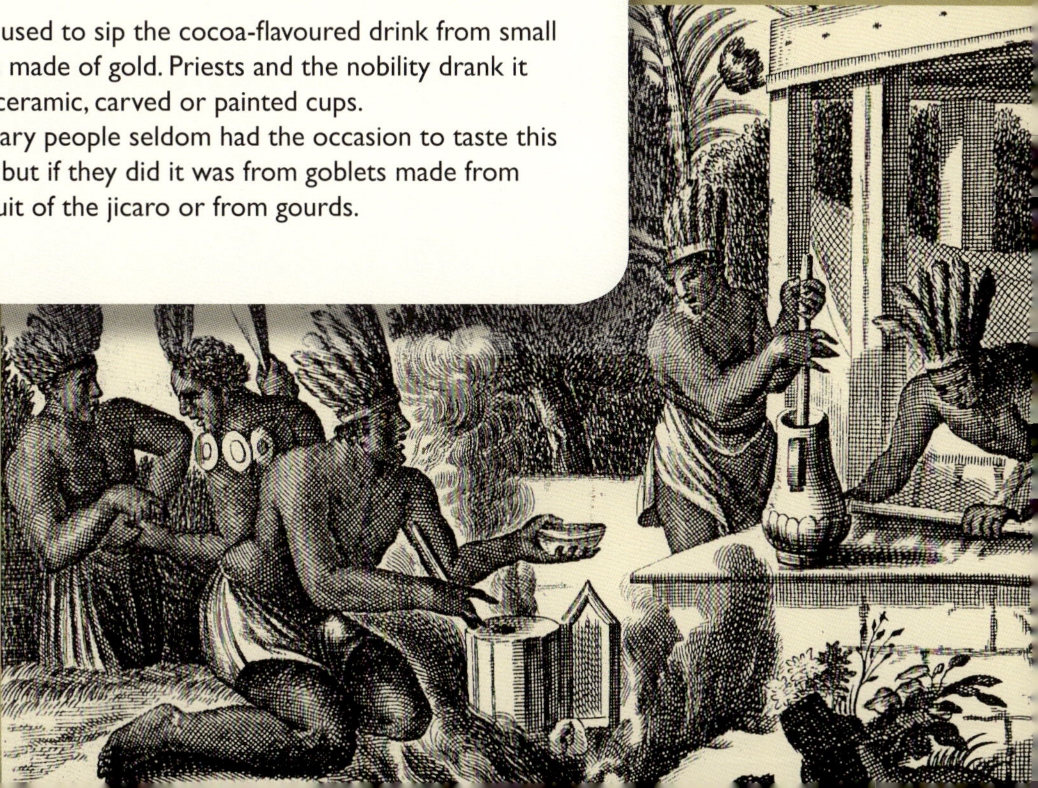

Using cocoa beans as a currency

In Central America, cocoa was a rare and therefore precious foodstuff.

This is probably the reason why the cocoa bean was used as a means of exchange in ancient times and then later as a currency in its own right.

You could buy a rabbit for 10 cocoa beans and a slave in good health would cost you 100 beans.

The Mayan numeration system was based on the number twenty. The standard measure the Mayas used was the carga; it was equivalent to the load one man could carry, that is 24,000 cocoa beans.

There were three types of currency: cocoa beans, volcanic rock or obsidian and copper in the shape of an axe or a knife.

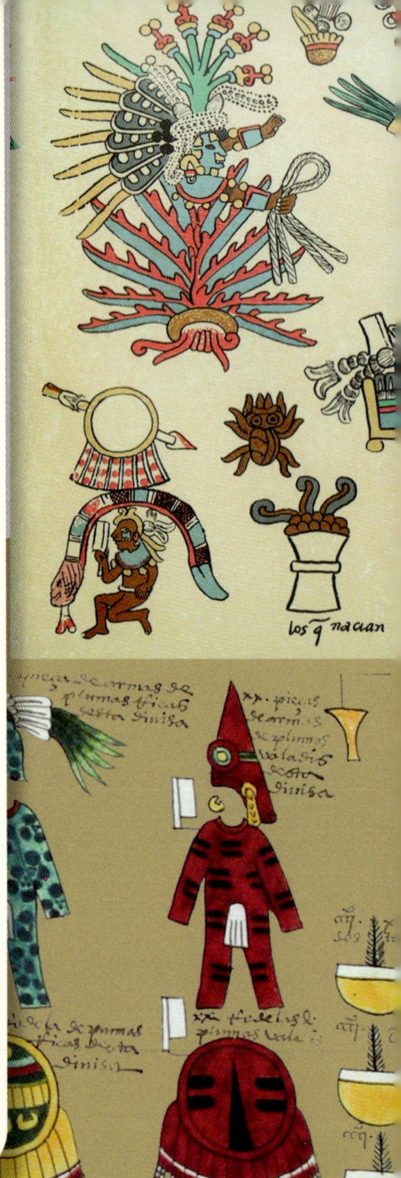

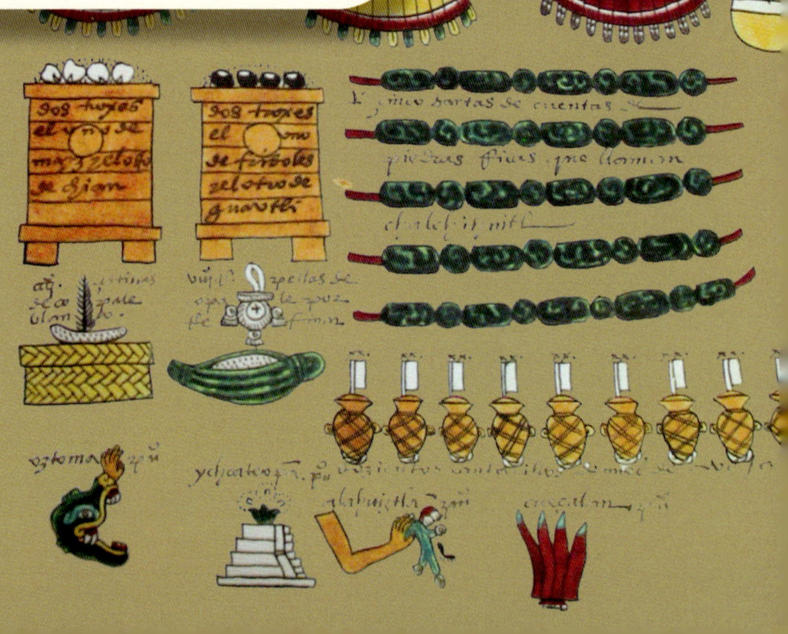

Codex Mendoza

The cocoa glyph and Codex

The word cocoa derives from the Olmec word ka-kaw.

Maya writing was highly evolved. The Mayas used logograms and each sign was associated with a syllable. By combining them into glyphs they composed words that could easily express abstract concepts.
They also wrote phonetically, which is not the case with most of our languages today.

The Mayas, and later on the Aztecs, liked to write descriptions of the way of life of their royal family and their people and they made these writings into books (codex) in the form of an accordion. They would sometimes use parchment made out of deer skin or a sort of paper made from cactus fibres. More often though they used the bark of a ficus tree called amatl.

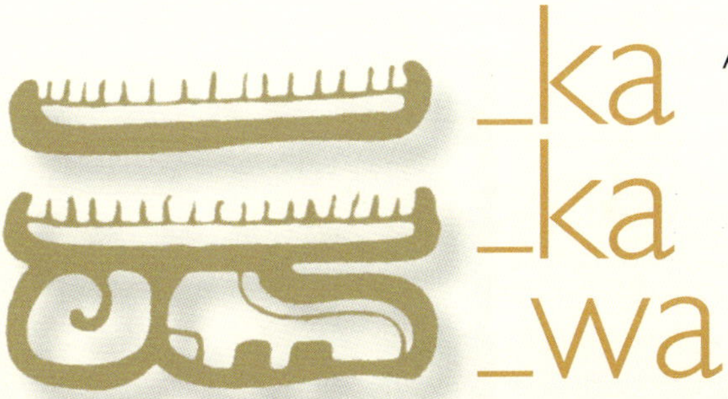

Aztec writing

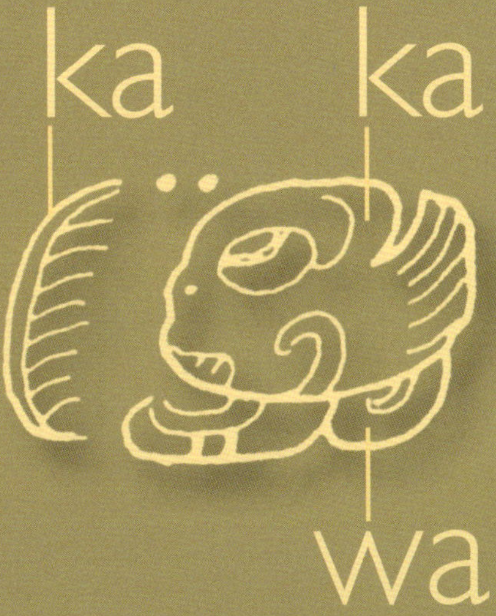

Maya writing

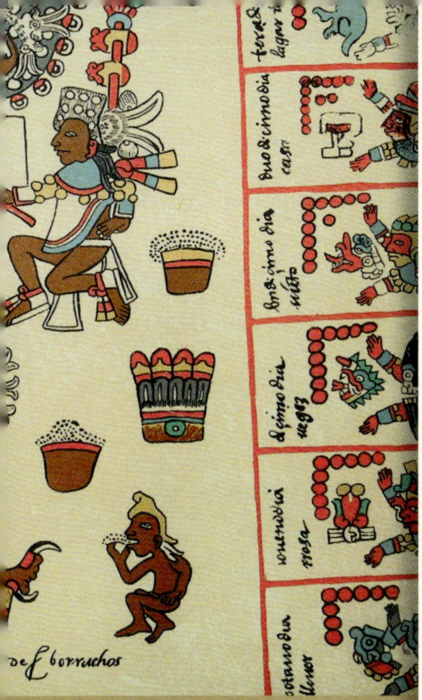

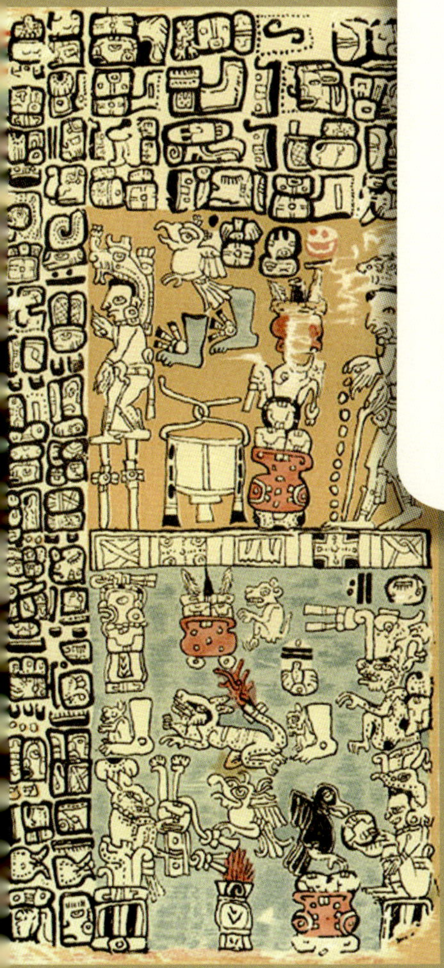

Codex Dresden

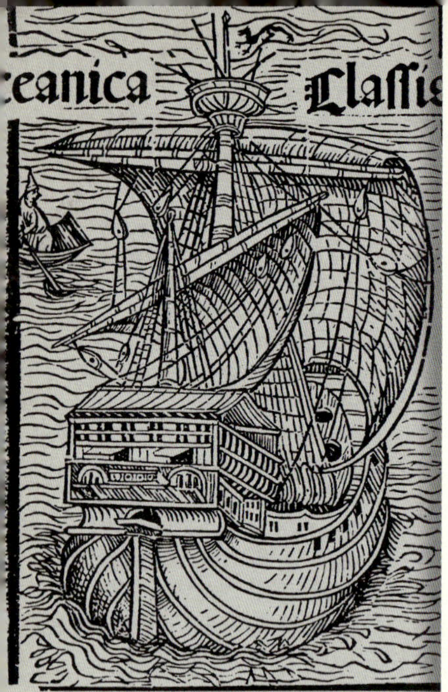

The arrival of the Spaniards

For many years, King Montezuma and his people had been waiting for the return of Quetzalcóatl, a God in the form of a feathered serpent. He had been banished by a high priest who was displeased by his great powers.

Cortez landed in Mexico on 21st April 1519.

When messengers came to warn king Montezuma that a man had landed, coming from the east, wearing a beard and shining scales (his armour) and bearing the sign of the four directions (the Cross), Montezuma believed that Quetzalcóatl had returned at last.

Cortez was received with full honours and was given a cocoa-flavoured drink in a golden cup to savour. Unfortunately this gesture proved fatal for the Indians, as it only served to increase the desire of the Spanish to plunder their gold.

Cortez meets Moctezuma
lithography 19th century

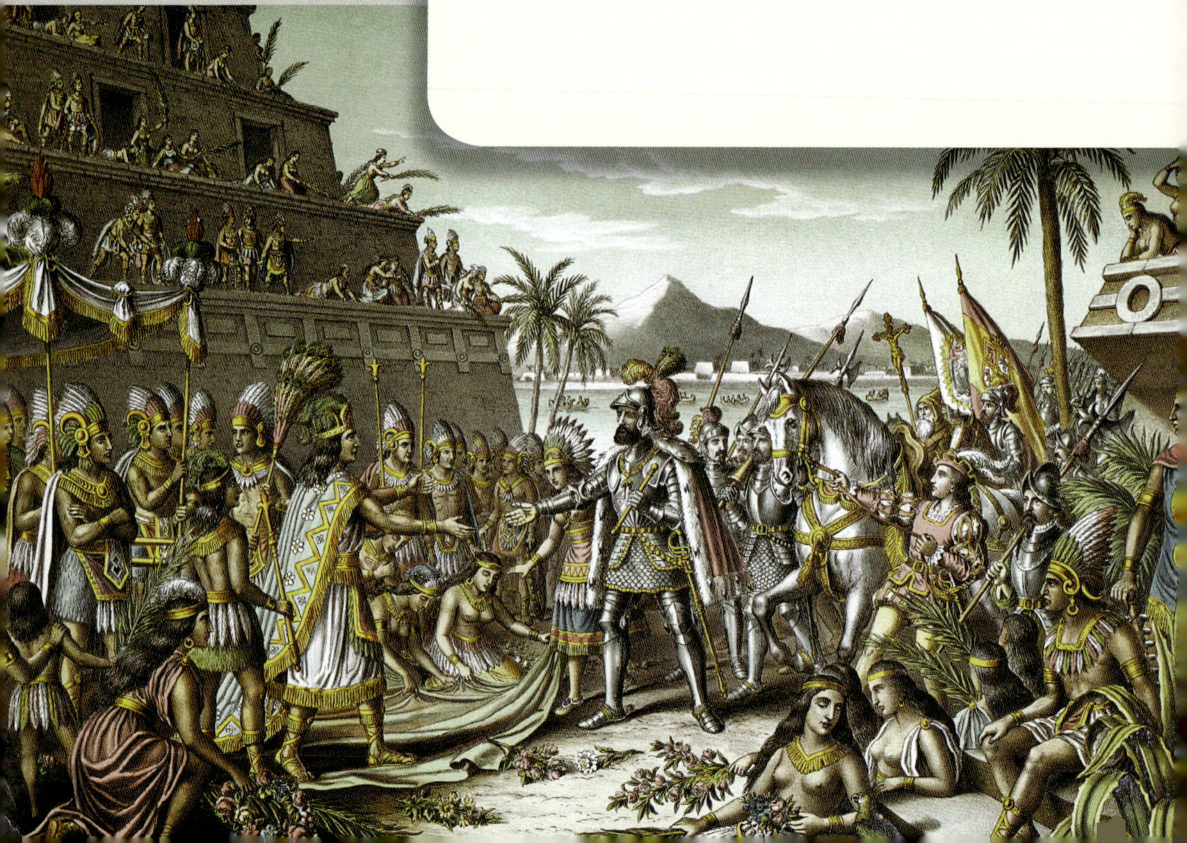

Cortez

It did not take long for Cortez to conquer the Aztec kingdom. Not only by using the firearms, cannons and horses he had brought with him but also by making the Indian tribes (who were the Aztecs' enemies) his allies.

In the meantime, Cortez and his men learned to appreciate their cocoa-flavoured drink. In a letter to Charles V in 1520 Cortez wrote: 'Cocoa beans are like almonds. The Indians use them as currency and to make a drink that gives them great strength and
prevents them from feeling tired'.

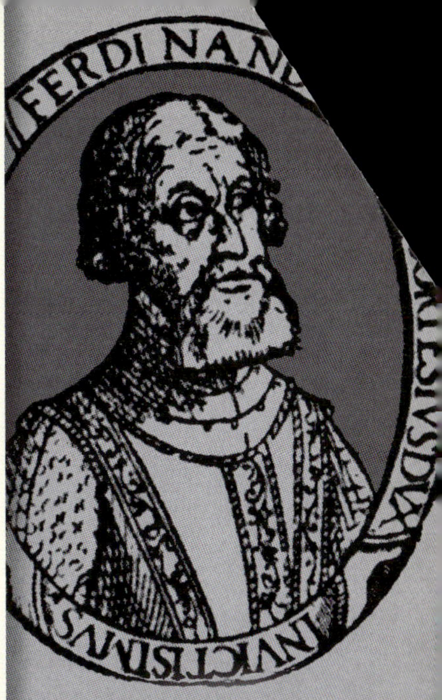

Colombus departs from the port of Palos destination India, but discovers America instead, Ricardo Balaca

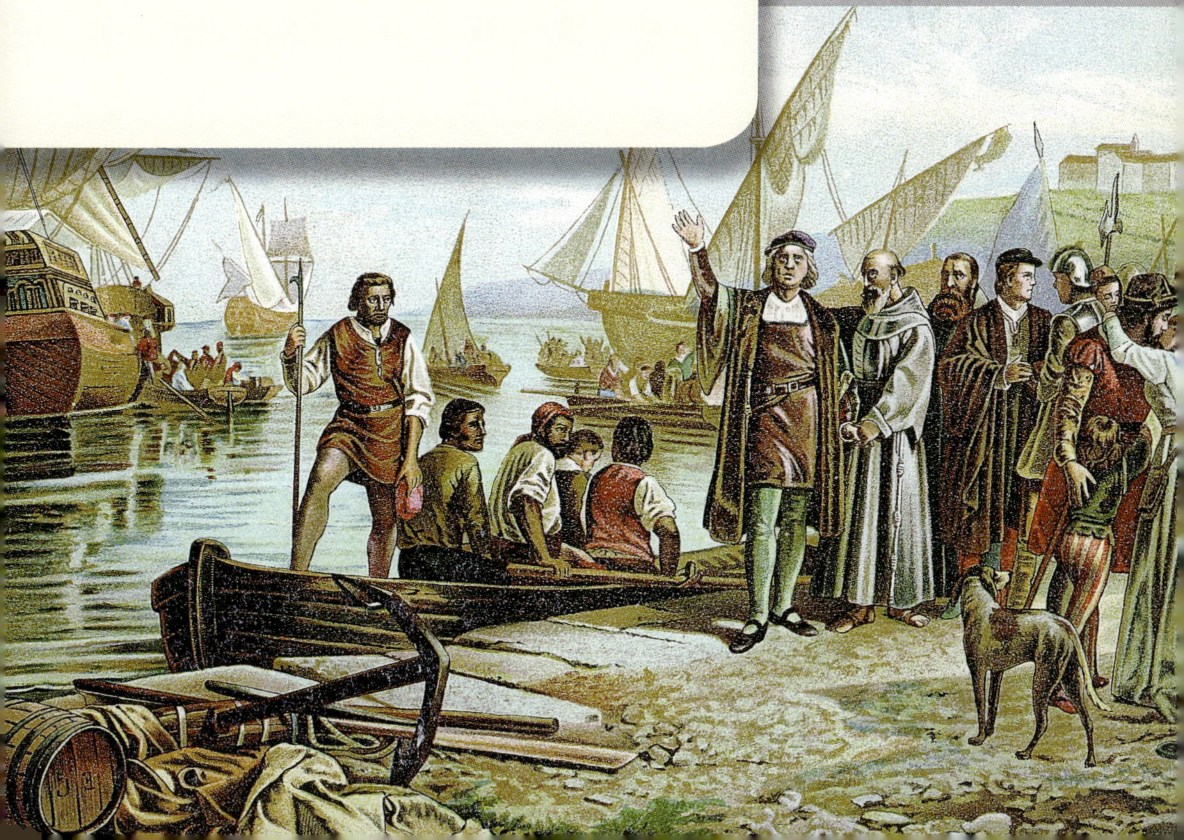

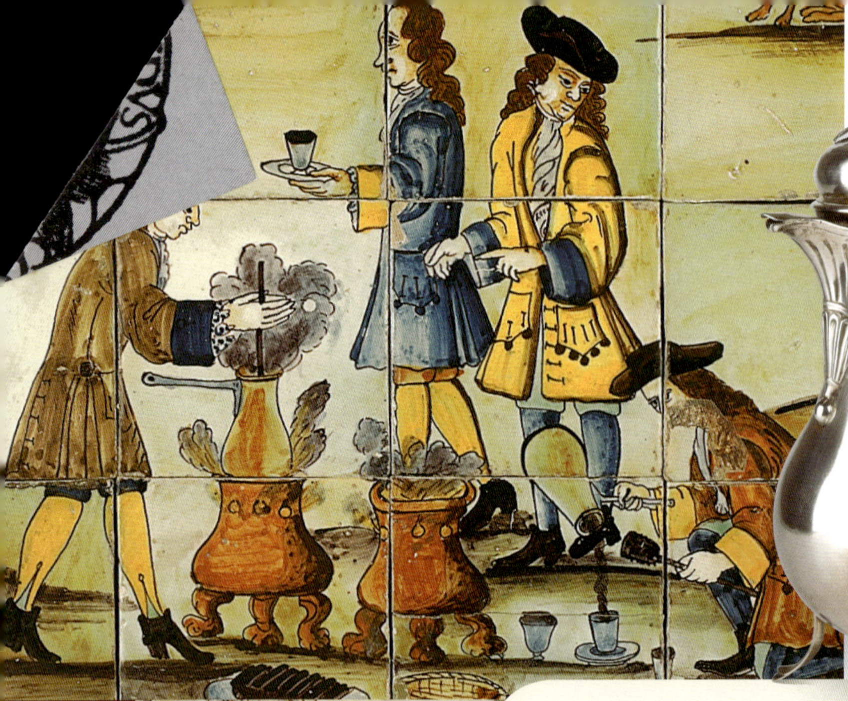

The Xocolatada, 1720, Barcelona, Museu de Ceràmica

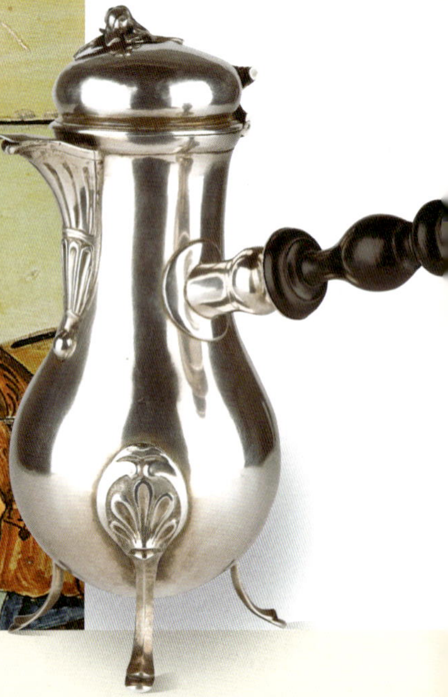

The cocoa-flavoured drink becomes a favourite with the Spanish

It is believed that it was the nuns of Oaxaca who were the first to start adding sugar to the cocoa-flavoured drink.

The Spanish ladies who had emigrated to Mexico enjoyed the cocoa-flavoured beverage so much that they could not stop drinking it.

For many years the Spanish who lived in Mexico kept the recipe for the drink secret.

It was only around 1528 that Cortez went back to Spain with a cargo of cocoa beans and the material necessary to make this cocoa-flavoured drink.

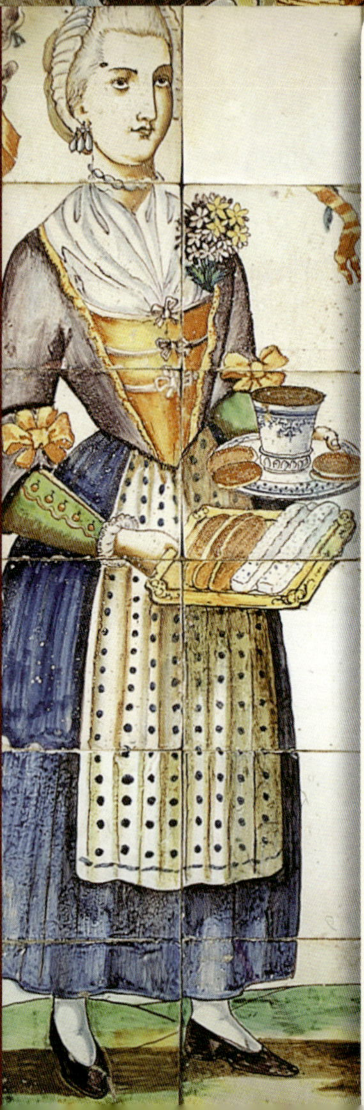

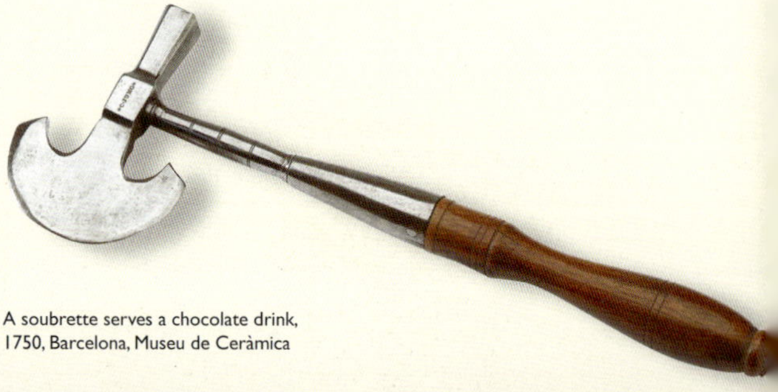

A soubrette serves a chocolate drink, 1750, Barcelona, Museu de Ceràmica

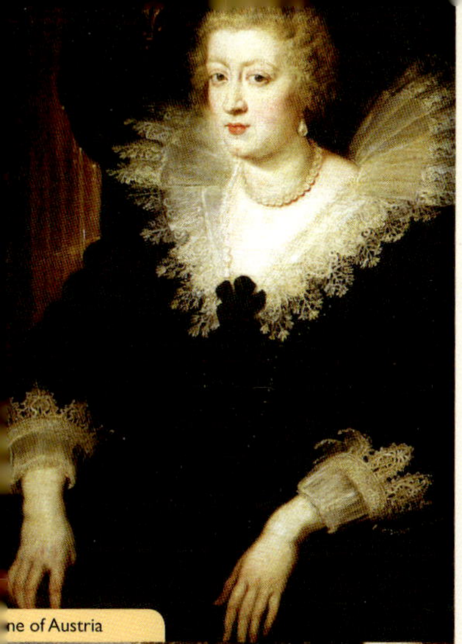

ne of Austria

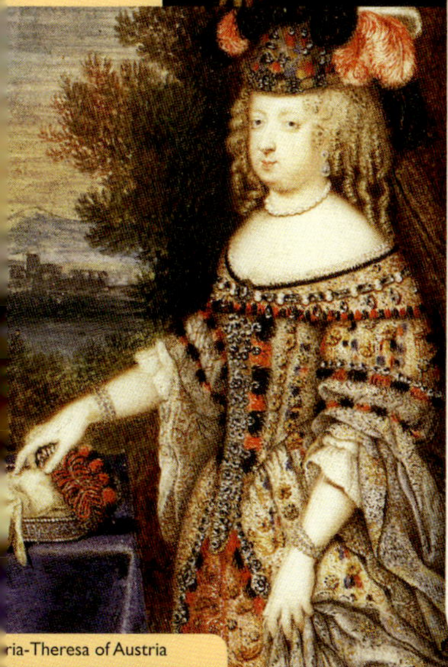

ria-Theresa of Austria

The cocoa-flavoured drink becomes widespread throughout Europe

Gradually the consumption of this sweetened cocoa-flavoured drink spread throughout the European continent in the wake of trade and cultural relations, but also as a result of several royal weddings. In France the drink appeared for the first time at the beginning of the 17th century.

Anne of Austria, daughter of Philip III, King of Spain, married Louis XIII in 1615 and went to live in France. She was accompanied by her personal molina, a servant who was expert in the preparation of the cocoa drink. Maria-Theresa of Austria, daughter of Philip IV of Spain, who was married to Louis XIV, was also extremely partial to this beverage.

Gradually the consumption of cocoa-flavoured drinks became a custom at the royal courts.
However, chocolate was expensive. At the end of the 18th century, a pound of chocolate (500 gr) was the equivalent of 5 days pay for a labourer.

The chocolate cup – The family of count de Penthièvre, Jean-Baptiste Charpentier, Musée de Chaalis

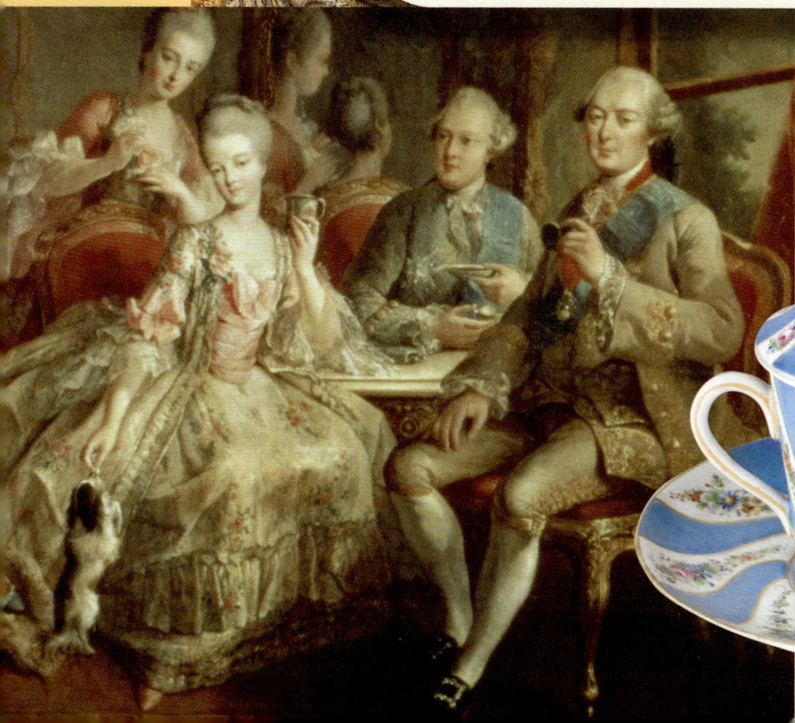

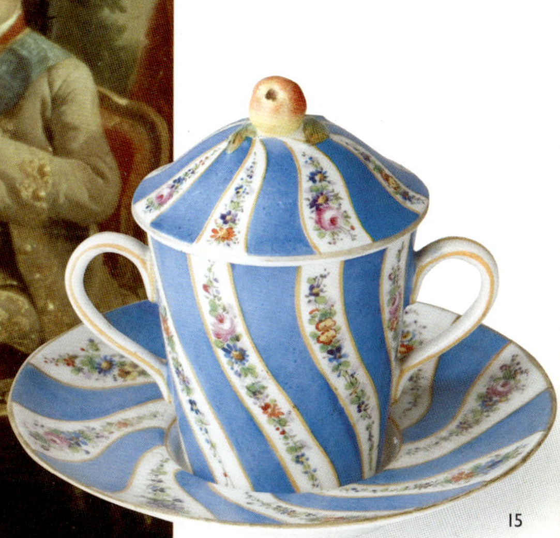

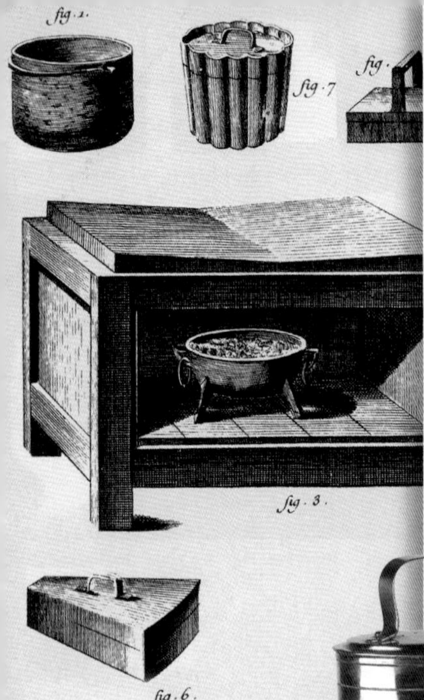

The production of cocoa paste between 1600 and 1800

The cocoa beans were delivered from the colonies already fermented and dried.
The European chocolate-makers roasted and winnowed the beans and turned them into a paste.

It was hard work doing this job. The only tool available was the traditional metate which was heavy to use and under which a heater was placed to soften the cocoa butter in order to obtain a smooth paste.

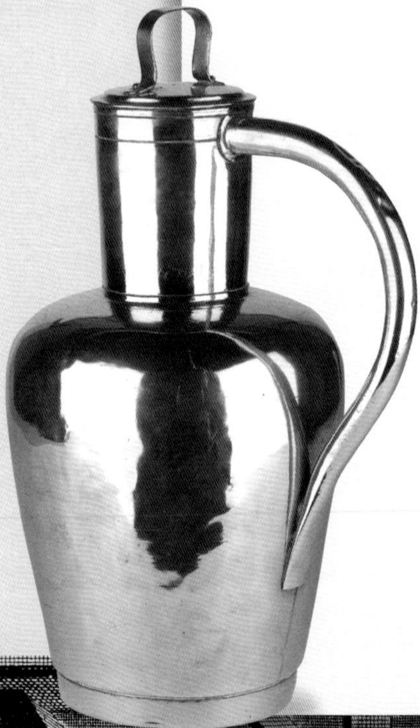

The worker was obliged to carry out his task bent double over a heated stone. The amount produced in one day was low.

The cocoa mass was then rolled out in sausage shapes and dried.
In this way it could be grated and diluted in hot water to make cocoa drinks.

Various other ingredients were added such as sugar, cloves, pepper, vanilla, cinnamon, hazel nuts and almonds.

The grinding of the cocoa beans on a heated grindingstone, *Le bon usage du Thé, du Café et du Chocolat,* de Blégny, Paris, 1687

Chocolate maker
Encyclopédie Diderot et d'Alembert

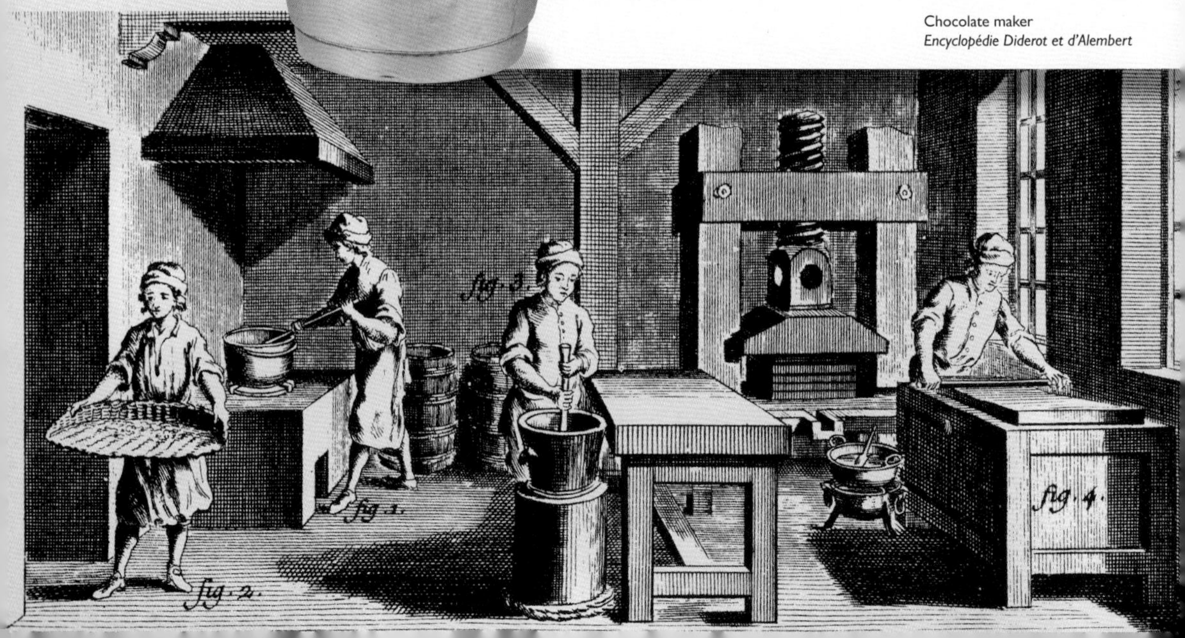

In the 19th century

The consumption of cocoa-flavoured drinks became popular all over Europe; at least as far as the rich were concerned.

In 1860, Napoleon III declared: 'Cocoa is not a luxury product. Its constitutional and nutritive properties are unquestionable and as its taste and aroma delight the senses of smell and taste, I consider it a consumer product for the general public and will lift the tax on it'.

Moreover, the gradual use of steam meant that cocoa paste could be produced in much larger quantities.

These two factors brought about the reduction in the price of chocolate and made it accessible to a far greater number of consumers.

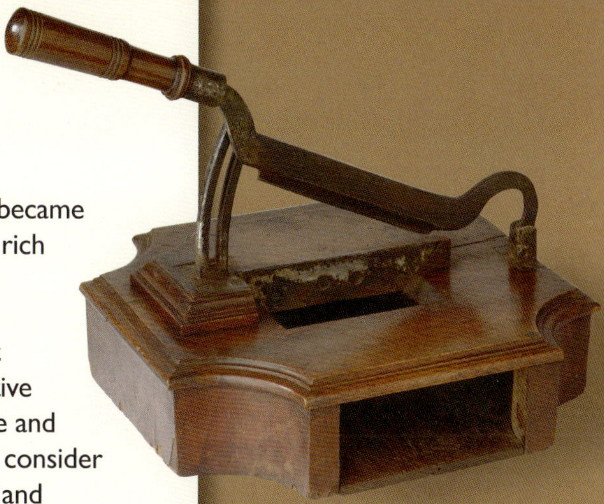

Fritsch, *Fabrication du chocolat*

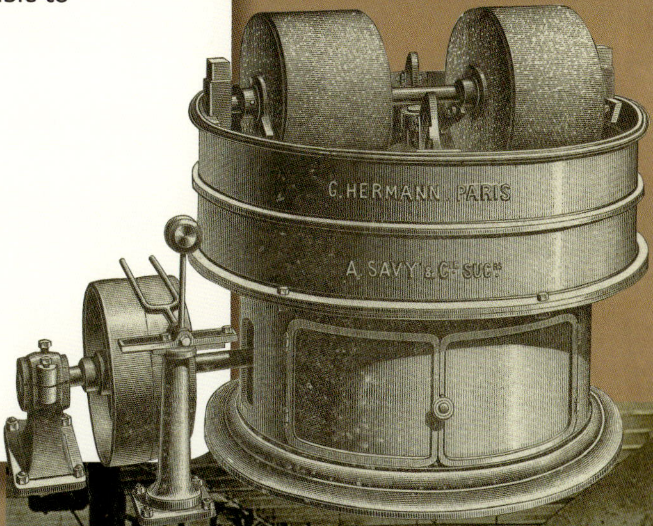

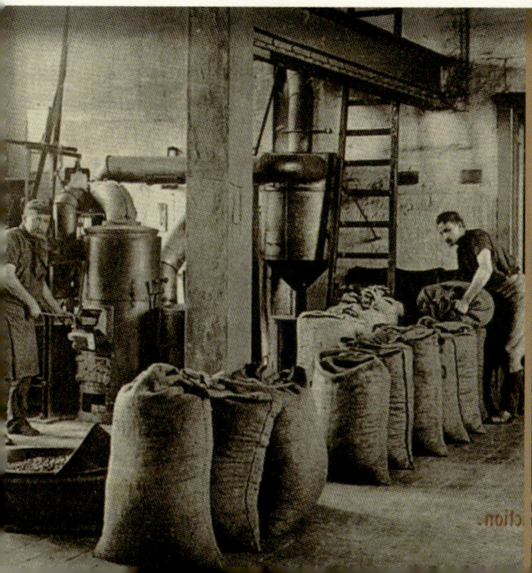

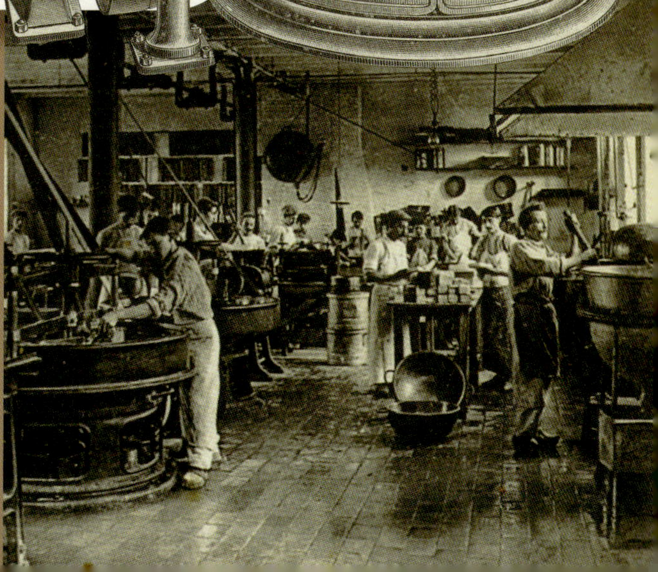

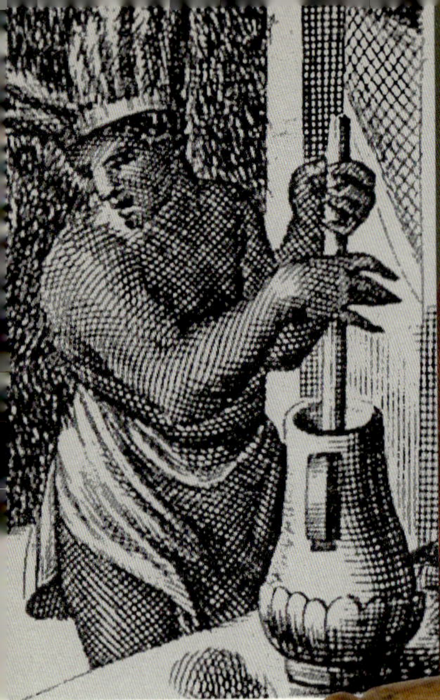

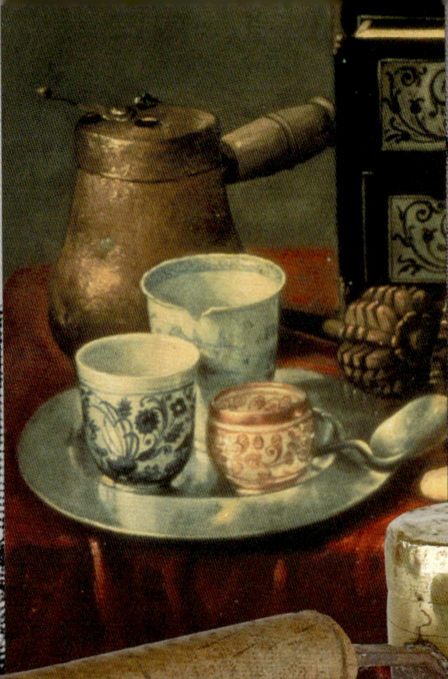

Antonio de Pereda y Salgado, 1652,
Ermitage in Saint-Petersburg,

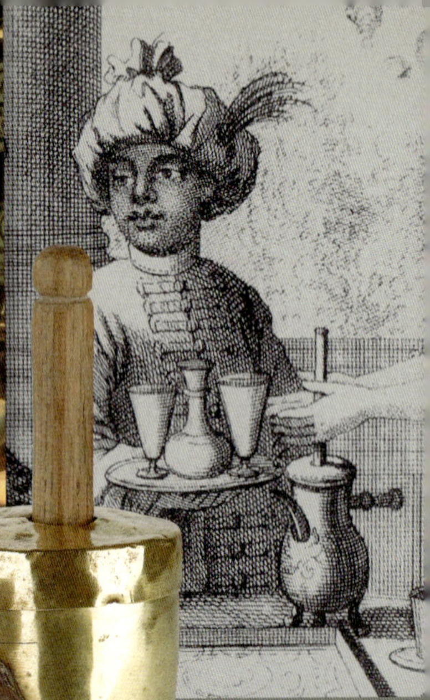

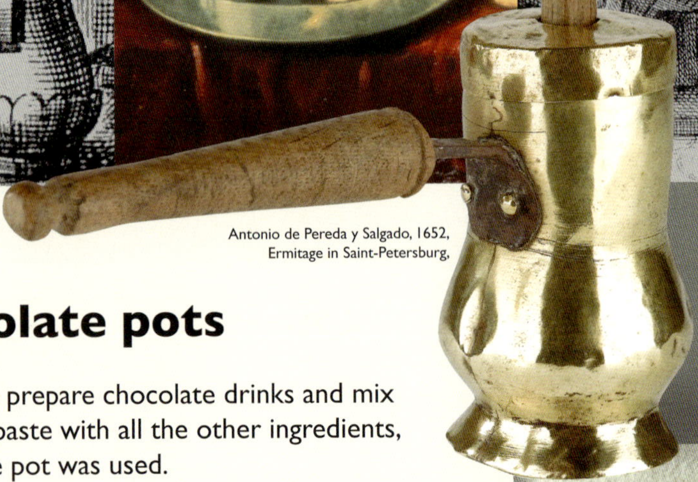

Chocolate pots

In order to prepare chocolate drinks and mix the cocoa paste with all the other ingredients, a chocolate pot was used.

The first chocolate pots were made out of iron or copper. Later on they became available in pewter and brass, and finally in porcelain, ceramic and especially in silver.

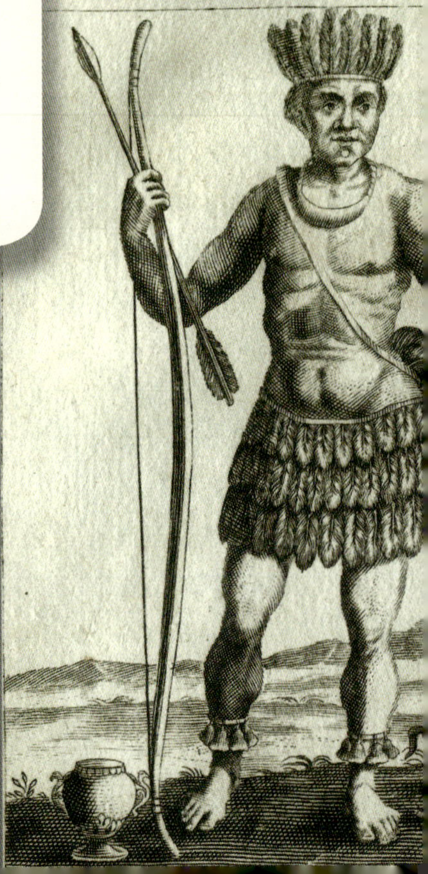

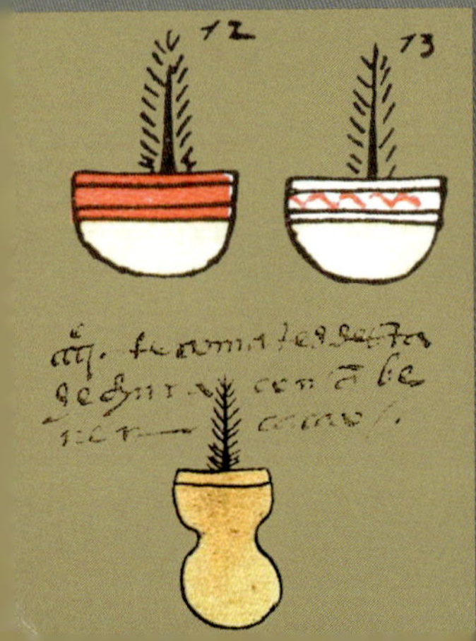

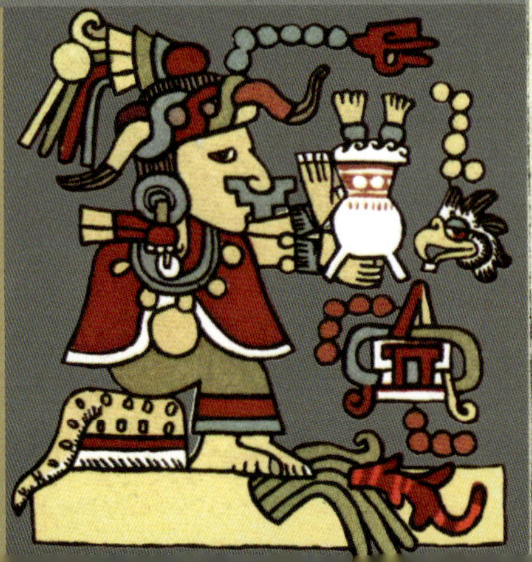

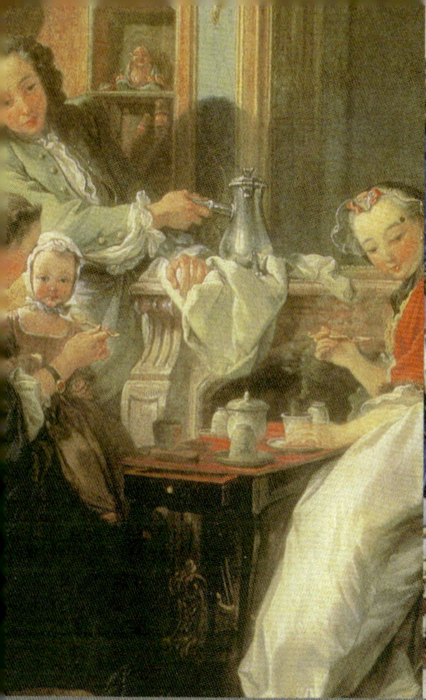

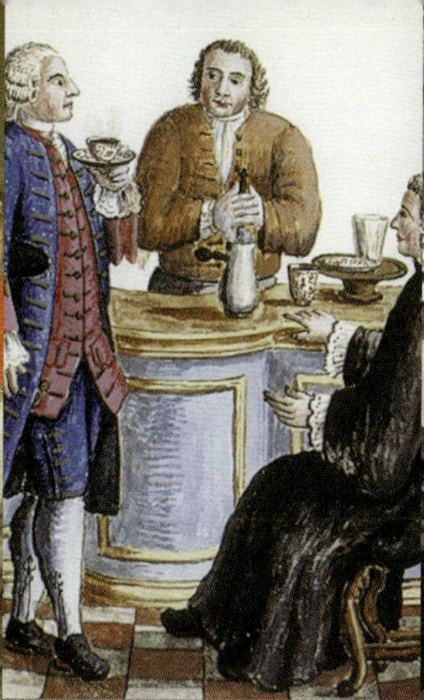

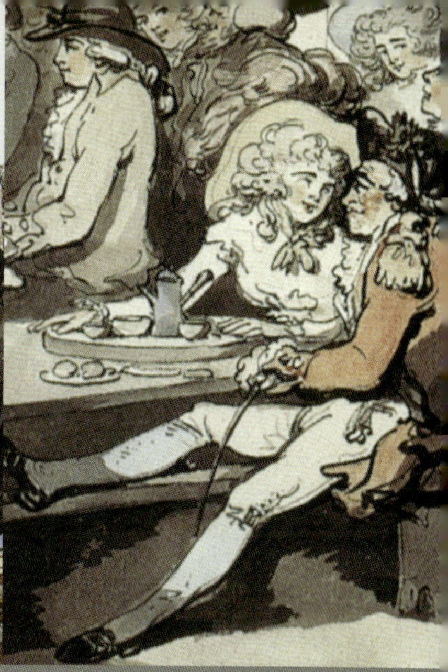

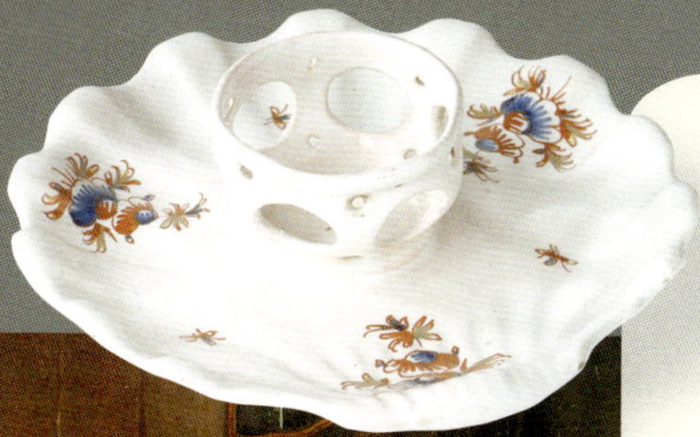

Chocolate cups

At the beginning of the 17th century, warm drinks such as coffee, tea and hot chocolate were not very popular and cups did not have handles which would prevent you from burning your fingers.

The mancerina was invented by the Marquis of Mancera, Viceroy of Mexico. The cup was held in a ring fixed to the saucer thus preventing it from being knocked over.
Some time later in France the trembleuse became fashionable. Here the cup was nestled in a hollow made in the saucer.

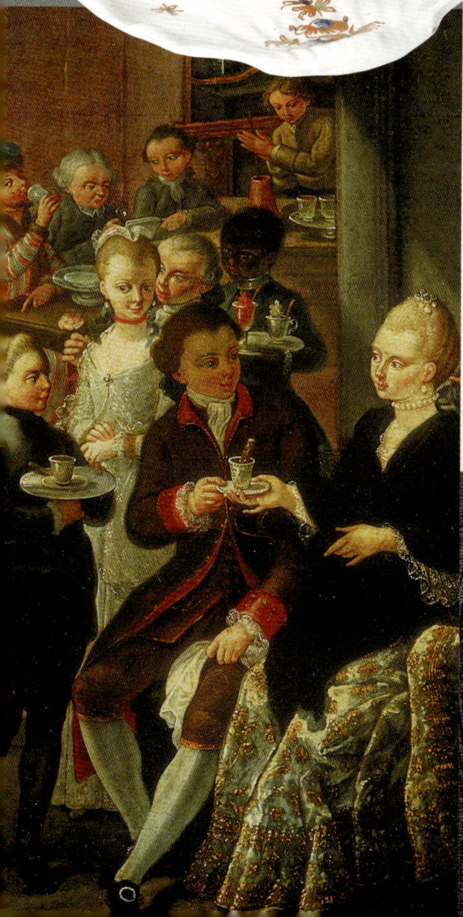

The chocolate drinker,
Louis-Marin Bonnel

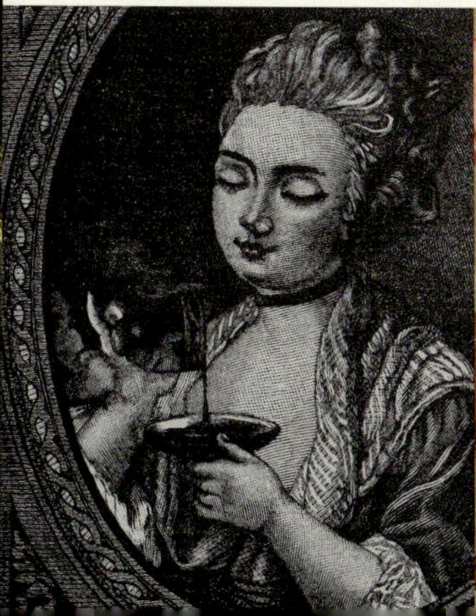

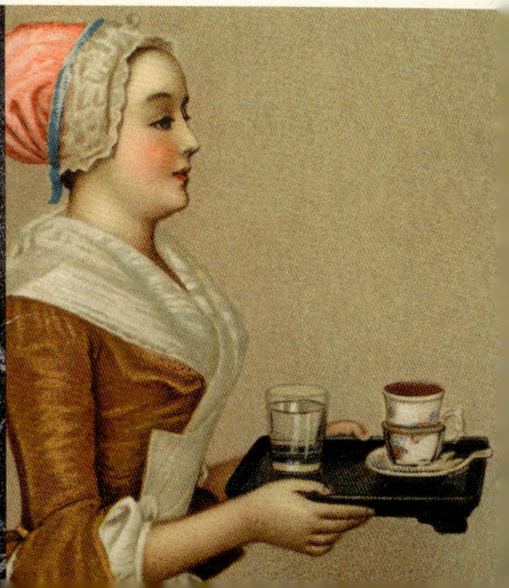

Chocolate

In 1825, Casper Van Houten discovered a technique for separating cocoa butter from the cocoa solids.

This meant that it was possible to blend cocoa butter with cocoa mass to make a mixture that was easy to turn out.

From then on it was possible to produce chocolate in bars for general consumption.

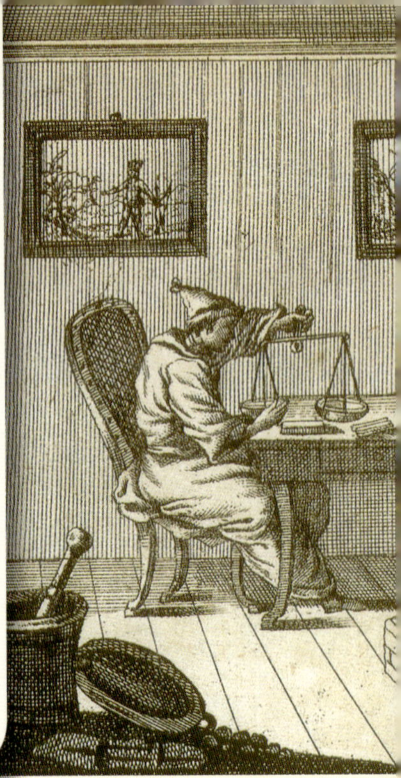

Chocolate production
Schauplatz de Natür und Künste

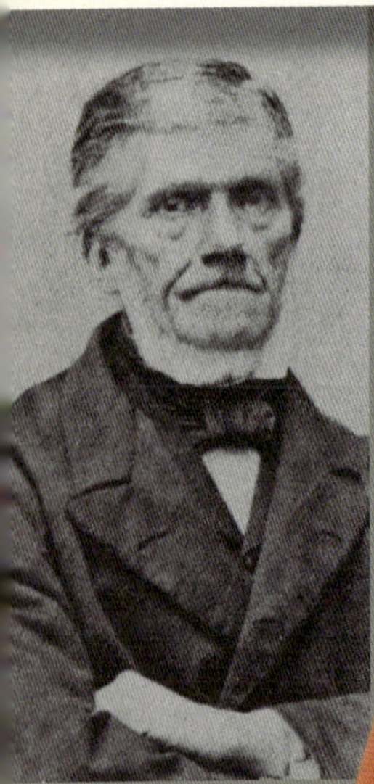

Casper Van Houten

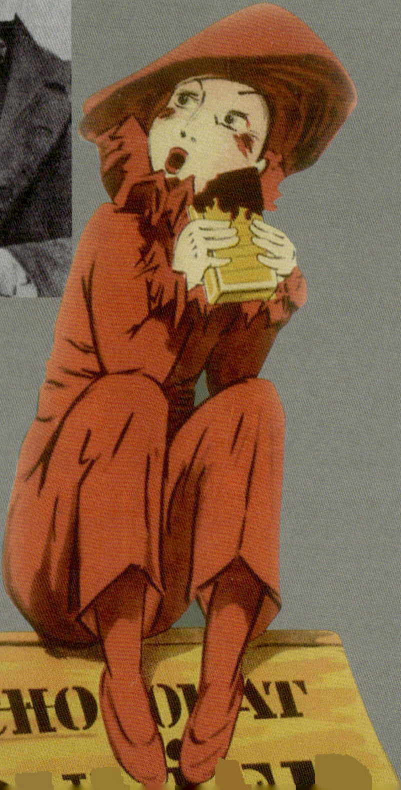

Dark Chocolate

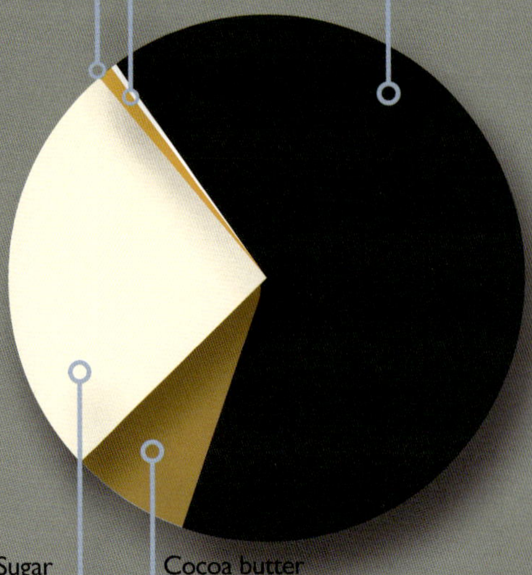

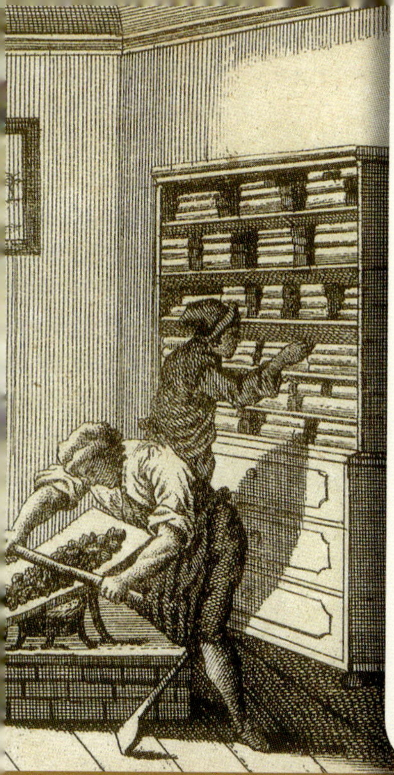

The ingredients of chocolate

Dark chocolate is made with cocoa mass, sugar and cocoa butter.

Milk chocolate is obtained by adding milk powder.

White chocolate is made from cocoa butter, sugar and milk powder.
This means that it contains one of the essential ingredients of cocoa, cocoa butter, and therefore it really is chocolate.

Milk Chocolate

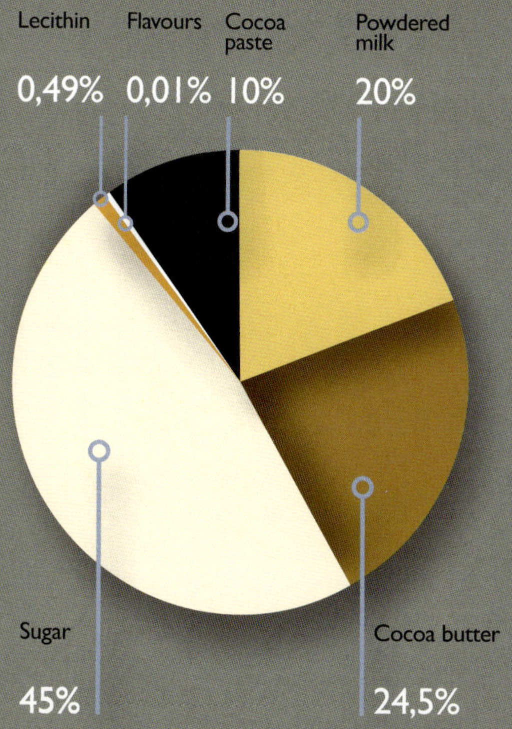

White Chocolate

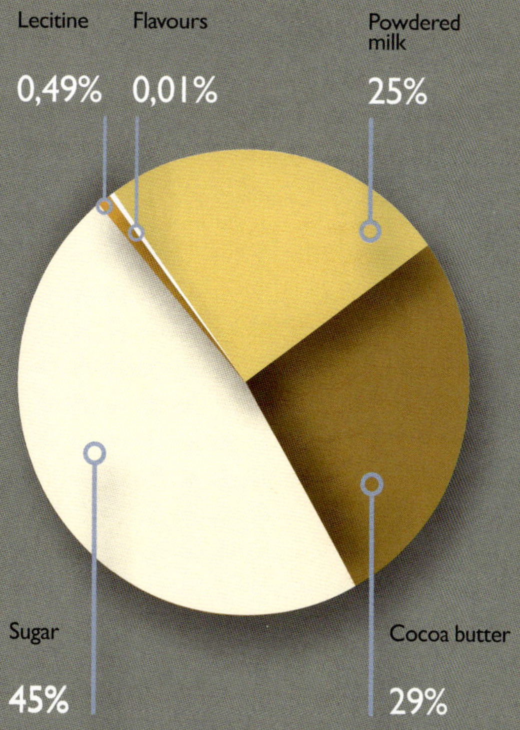

The production of chocolate

Making chocolate and especially high quality chocolate from cocoa beans is no easy matter. Above all you need to have good quality, well-fermented cocoa beans from a top variety of tree.

The beans are processed as follows:

Roasting
cocoa beans are roasted at a temperature of 200 to 250°C for 15 to 20 minutes.

Winnowing
once roasted, the cocoa beans are winnowed.

Grinding
the beans are ground and made into a paste.

Blending
according to the type of chocolate desired, the cocoa paste is blended with sugar, milk powder and cocoa butter in the required proportions.

Refining
the mixture is refined using cylinders. The longer the refining the finer the chocolate and the better the taste.

Conching
the refined chocolate is poured into a conch where it is heated and blended in order to get rid of any undesirable aromas.

Finally, the right viscosity
according to how the chocolate will be used it must be more or less runny. After adding a little cocoa butter or lecithin, the chocolate becomes even more delicious and is now ready to eat.

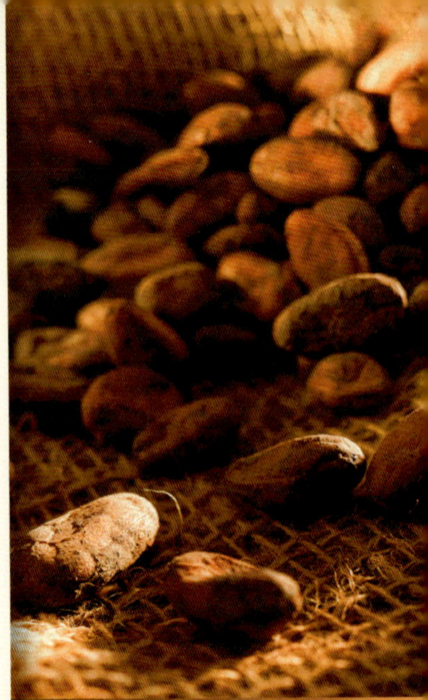

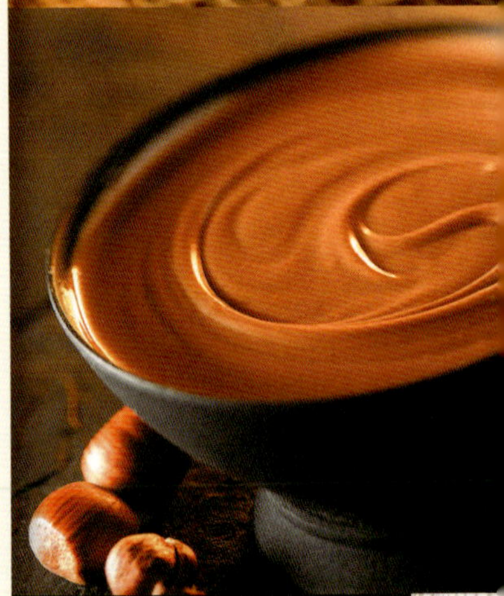

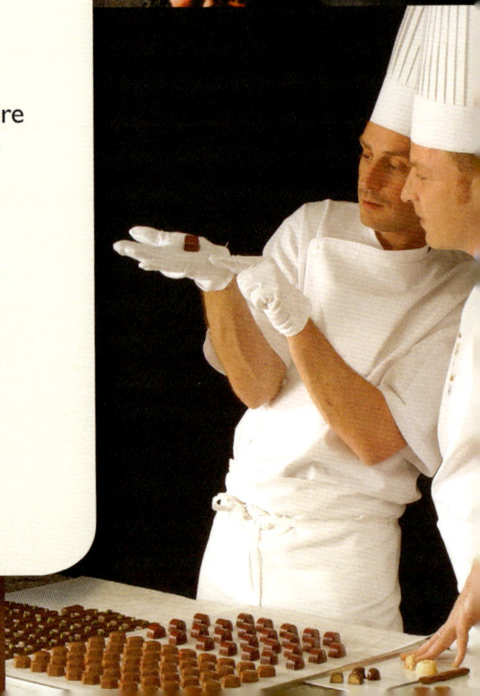

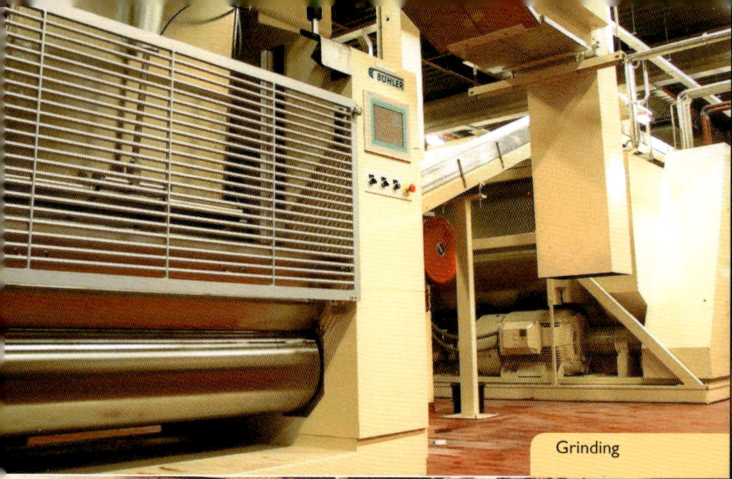
Grinding

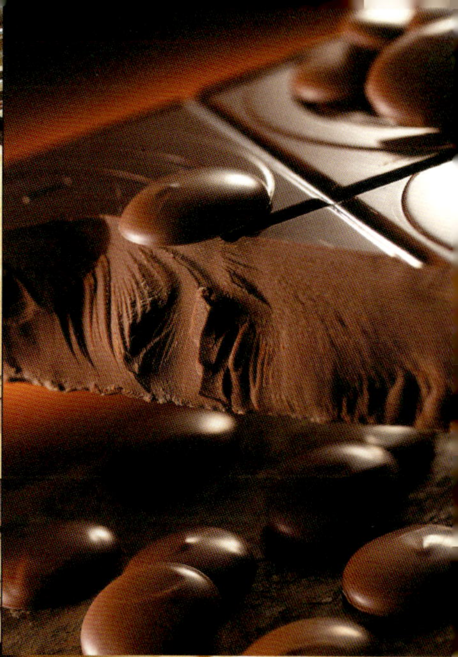

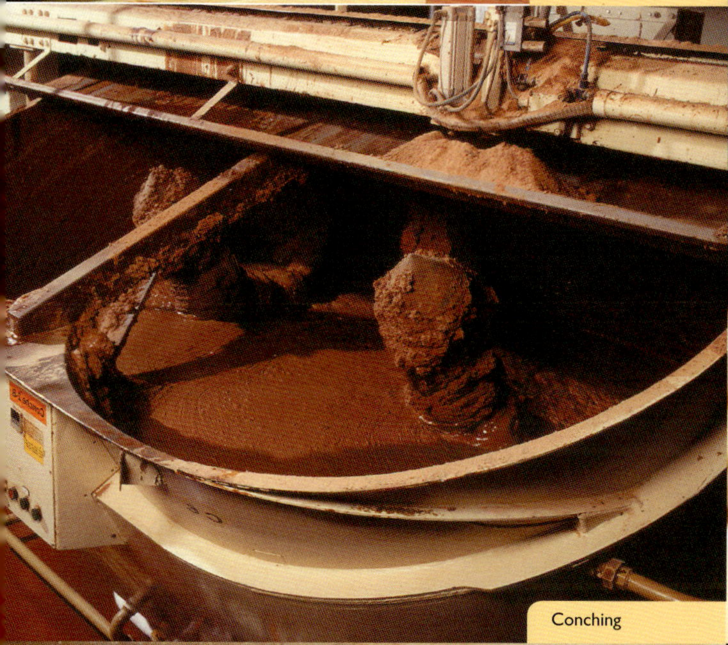
Conching

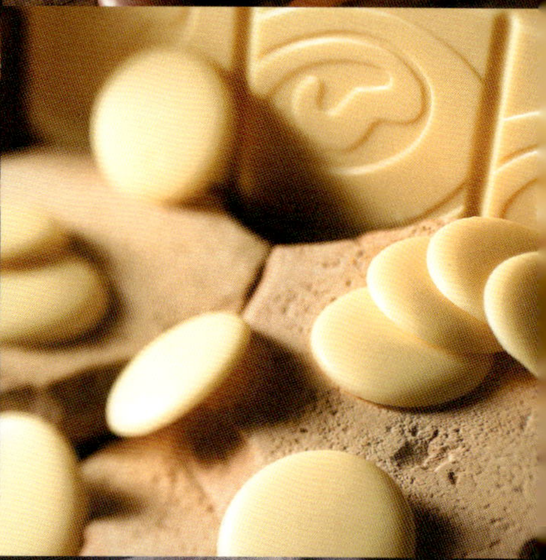

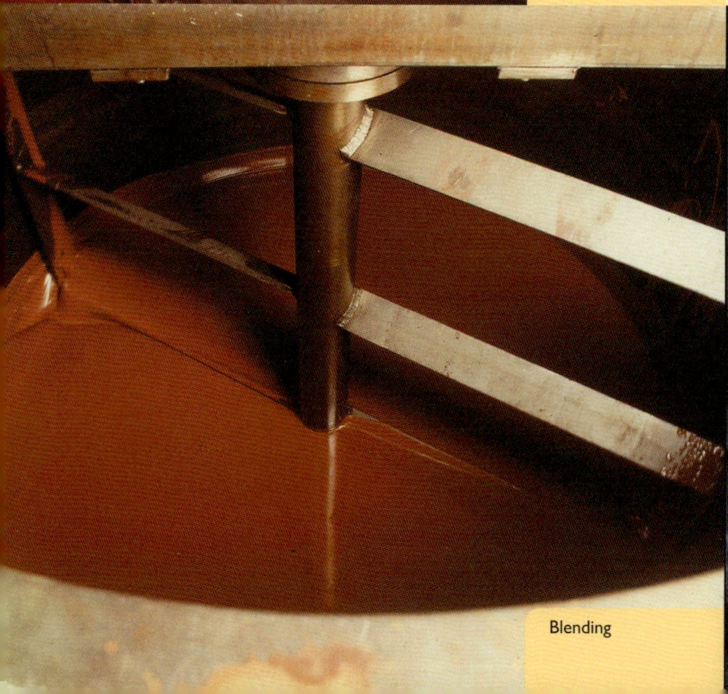
Blending

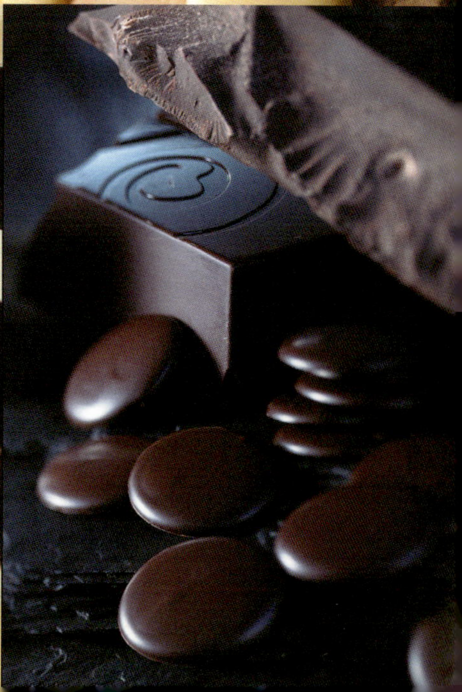

Praline chocolates

The word praline originated in France where it was first used by Mr Choiseul, Count of Plessis-Praslin who was a French marshal and diplomat in the 17th century. His cook created a new sweet consisting of a sugar-covered almond that was called praslin.

It was Jean Neuhaus who invented the praline in 1912. He filled a chocolate cup with ground sugar-coated nuts and called it praline.

Jean Neuhaus

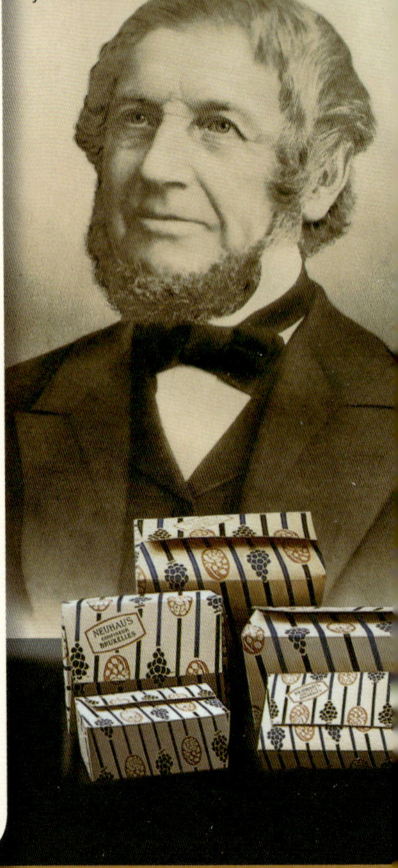

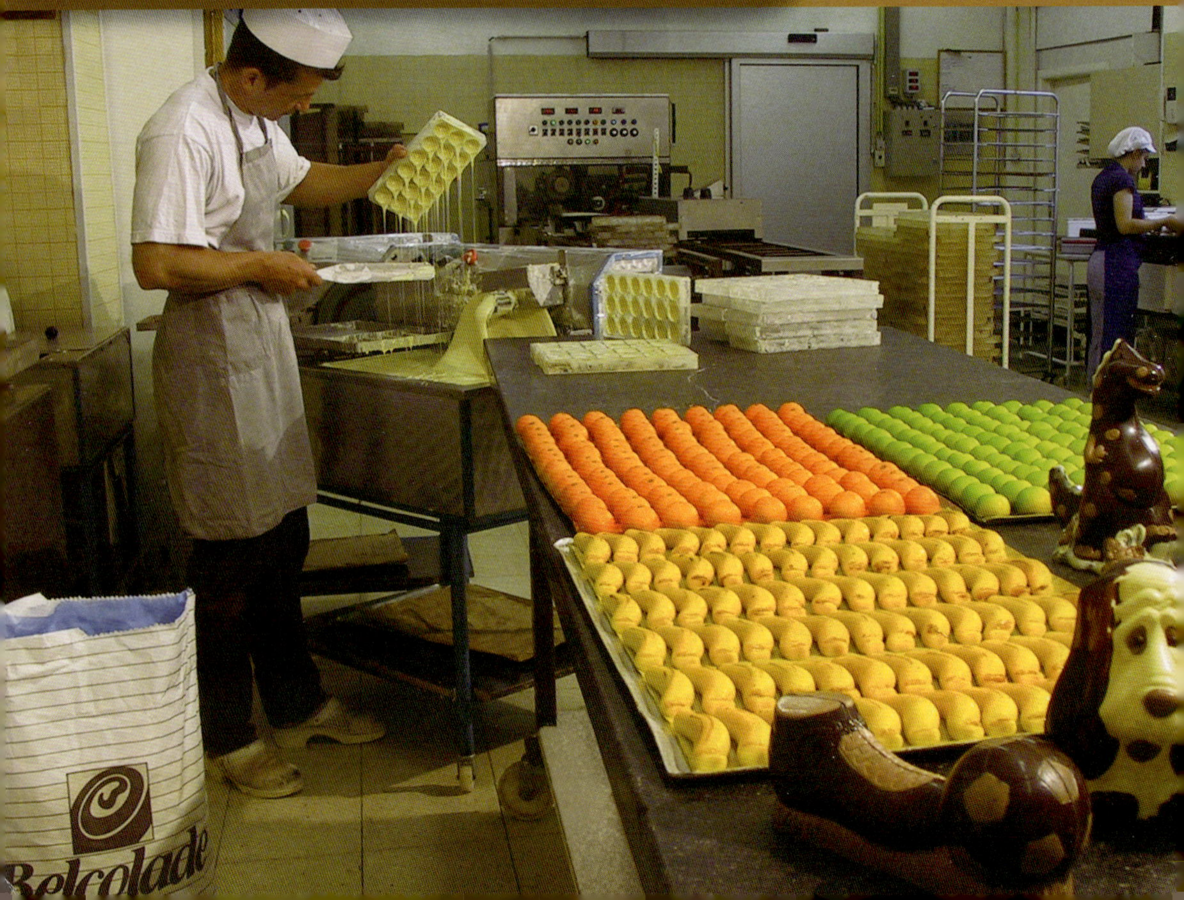

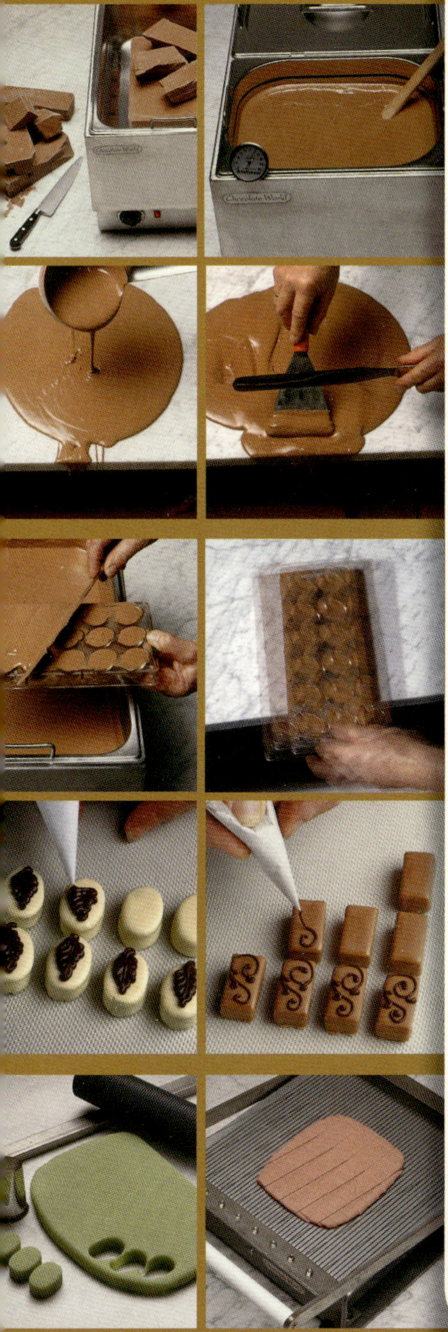

How chocolate sweets are made

Tempering chocolate

In order for chocolate products to be nice and shiny, the chocolate has to be correctly tempered. This process ensures that the crystals that form inside the chocolate when it is cooling down are small, regular and well-aligned.

The traditional method of tempering consists of pouring the melted chocolate on a marble slab and then smoothing it out with a spatula until its temperature has fallen to between 27°C and 28°C. Then the chocolate is heated again to a temperature of 29°C. This encourages the formation of small crystals of the same size in the chocolate and gives the best result.

How pralines are made

Melted chocolate is poured into a mould which is then turned over to remove the surplus. The bubbles of air are removed by making the mould vibrate. The moulds are left to cool until the chocolate becomes solid. The chocolate cups are filled and left to cool again before being covered by a thin layer of chocolate.

Coating

First the fillings, for example almond paste (marzipan), are cut into pieces, then each piece is dipped in melted chocolate and left to cool in a refrigerator.

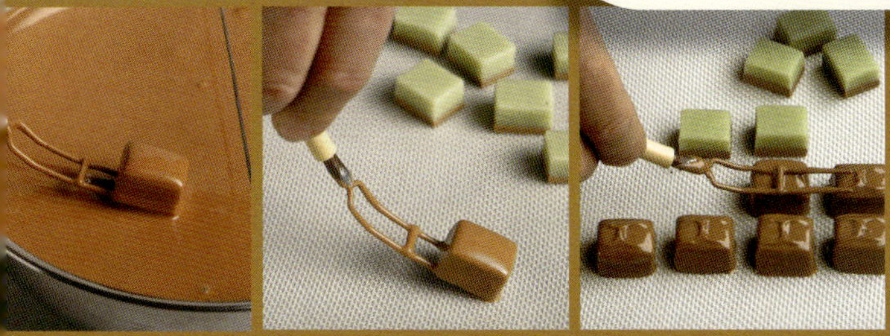

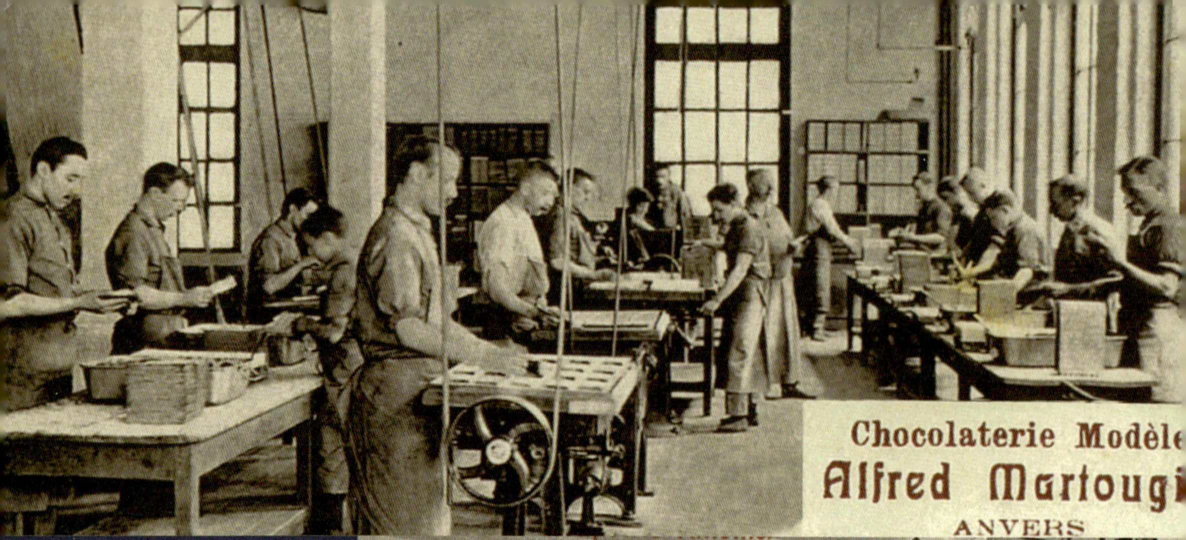
Chocolaterie Modèle
Alfred Martougi
ANVERS

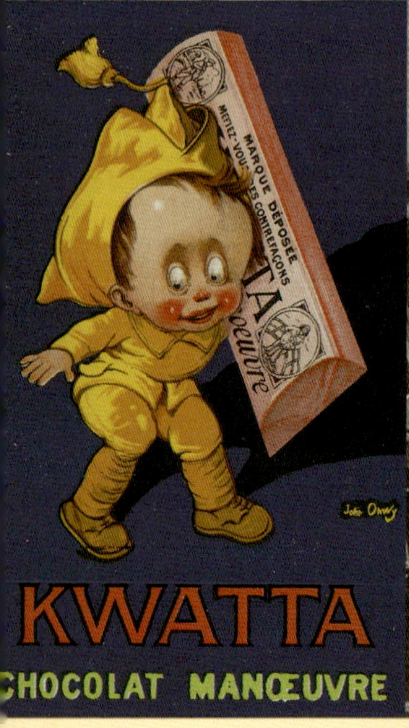
MARQUE DEPOSEE
KWATTA
CHOCOLAT MANŒUVRE

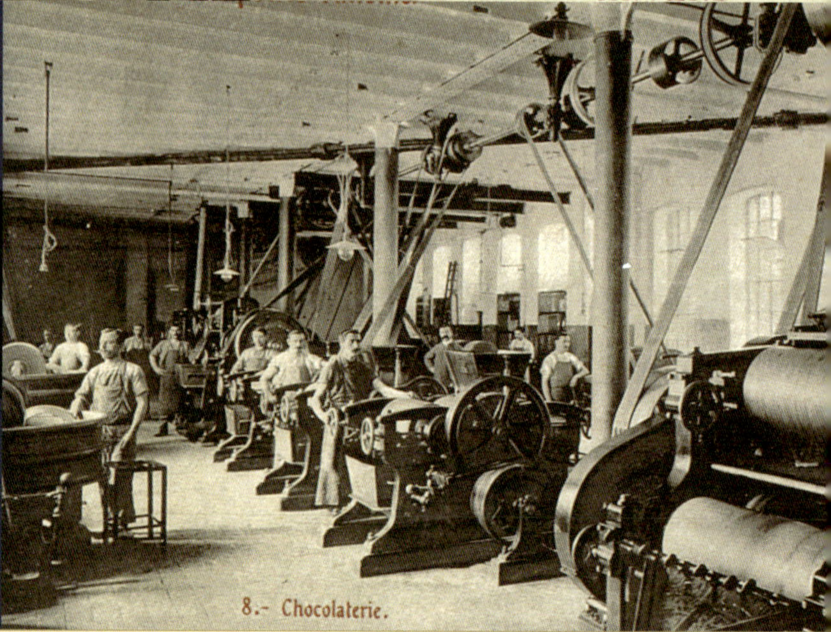
8.- Chocolaterie.

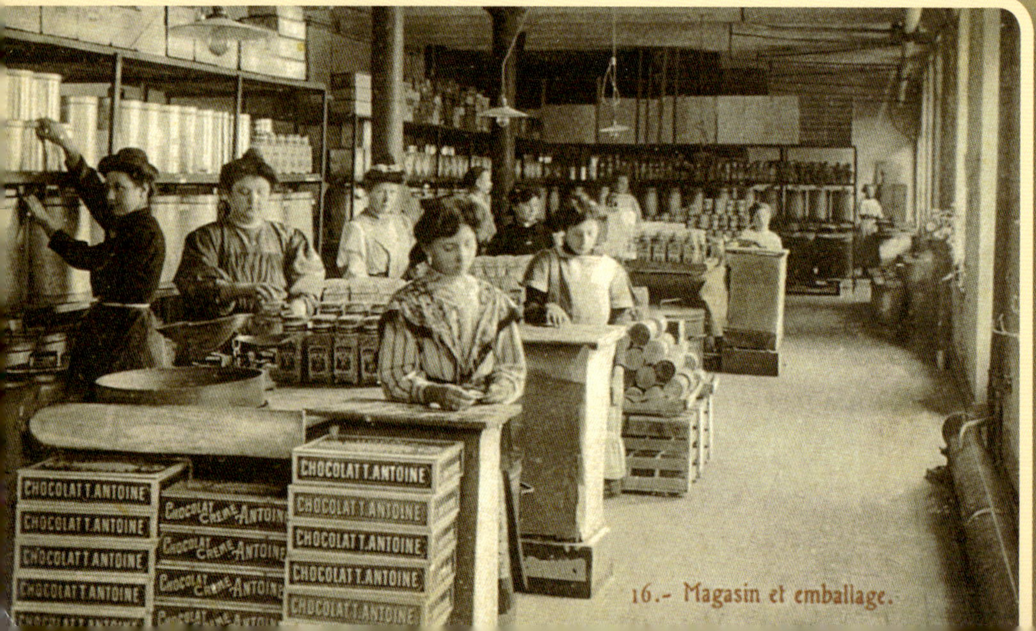
CHOCOLAT T. ANTOINE
16.- Magasin et emballage.

The history of chocolate in Belgium

Beginning of the 17th century

The first chocolate manufacturers saw the light of day at the beginning of the 17th century in what is now the country of Belgium.
Part of the area of Belgium was dominated by the Spanish and this is how cocoa-flavoured drinks were first introduced to our regions. At the time, chocolate was rare and expensive and was only sold in chemists' and tobacconists' shops.

The 19th century

In 1835 a steam engine was installed for the first time in a chocolate factory in Belgium. This meant that much greater quantities of cocoa beans could be ground.
In the early 1840s Bernaerts and Claret became well known in Brussels for their chocolate.

Towards the middle of the 19th century chocolate became a popular delicacy. It disappeared from the chemists' shops where it was mixed with certain medicines to disguise their bad taste to become a sweet in its own right.
Gradually new companies opened all over the place: G. Meurisse in Antwerp, N. de Launoy and A. Joveneaux in Tournai, Jean Neuhaus, Senez-Sturbelle and Demaret in Brussels.

By the end of the 19th century, chocolate-makers had multiplied. Martougin set up in Antwerp and Jacques in Verviers. The brand name Côte d'Or was registered in 1883 when Kwatta was just starting business.

The 20th century

Aiglon was establised in Verviers and Clovis, Saga Crista, Faucon, Decerf, Angenot-Hongresse and Manguette were also set up.
The chocolate industry developed new products that were widely advertised to make them known to the general public.

At last chocolate had become available for everybody, whatever their class in society.

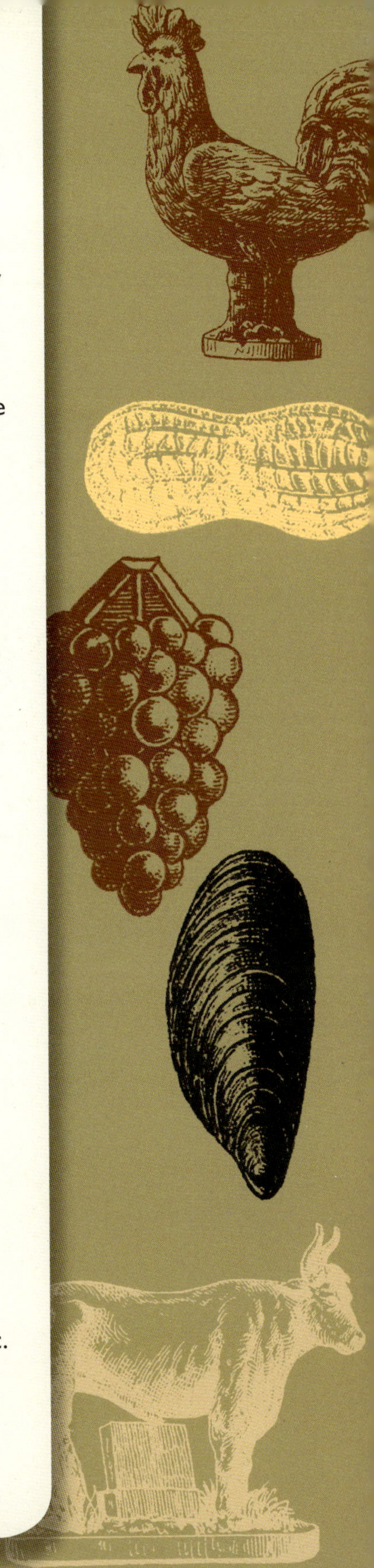

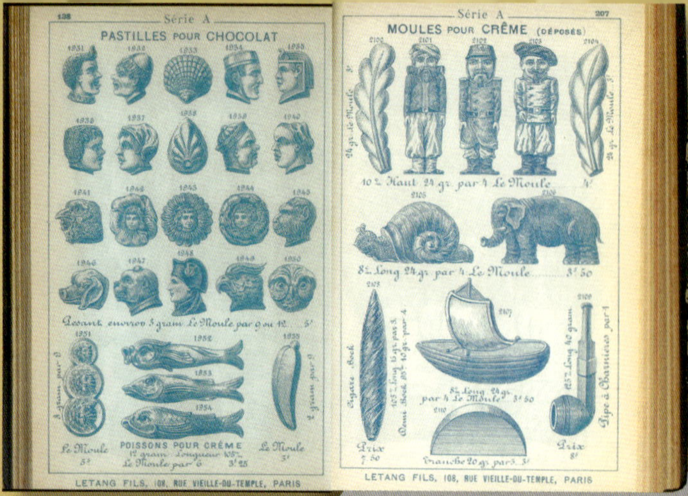

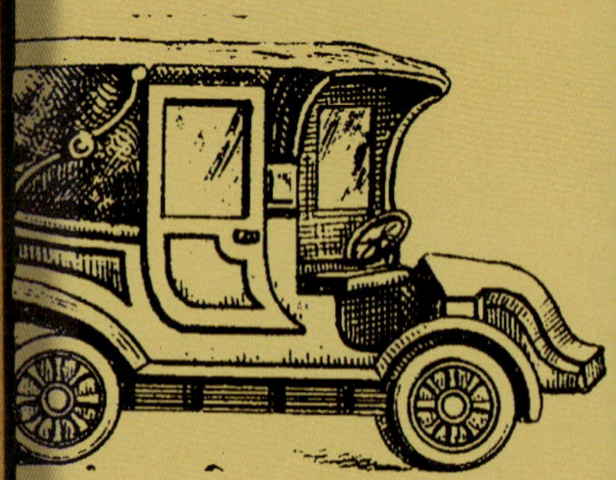

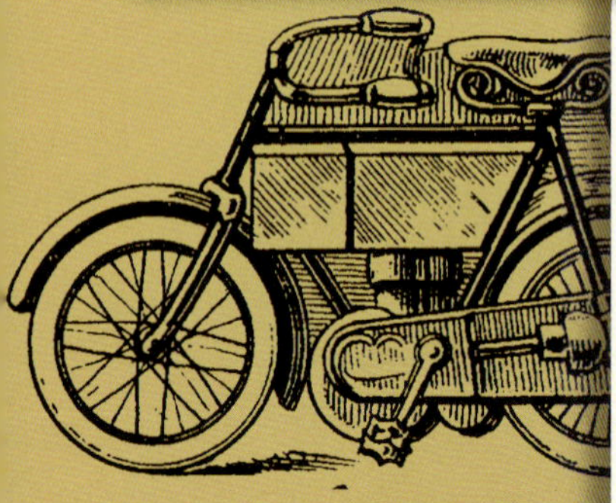

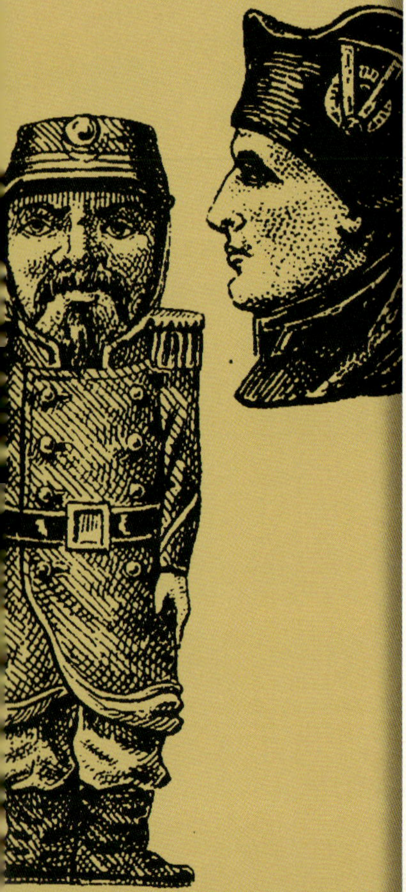

The history of chocolate in France

The 17th century

According to several sources, the first people to start making chocolate in France were the Jews who had fled Portugal and taken refuge in Bayonne.
1609 is the date most often mentioned, but to this day no written document has ever been found to confirm this.

On 28th May 1659, Louis XIV granted David Chaillon the exclusive right for a period of 29 years to 'produce and sell a mixture called chocolate, either as a liqueur, in drops or any other form that he pleases and to this end may import from foreign countries all the necessary ingredients that go into making this so-called chocolate'.

The 19th century

In 1800, Sulpice Debauve opened a shop, first in the rue Saint-Dominique and then in the rue des Saints-Pères. This marked the turning point when chocolate, that until then had only been sold in chemists' shops because of its therapeutic use, became available as a sweet.

In 1825 Jean Antoine-Brutus Menier, who used to make powders for the pharmaceutical industry, started making his own chocolate in Noisiel.

In 1847, Victor-August Poulain, a sweet-maker, came to live in Blois. In 1862 he opened a factory at la Villette where in 1872 he installed several steam engines. In 1893 he created a company called Poulain to manufacture chocolate.

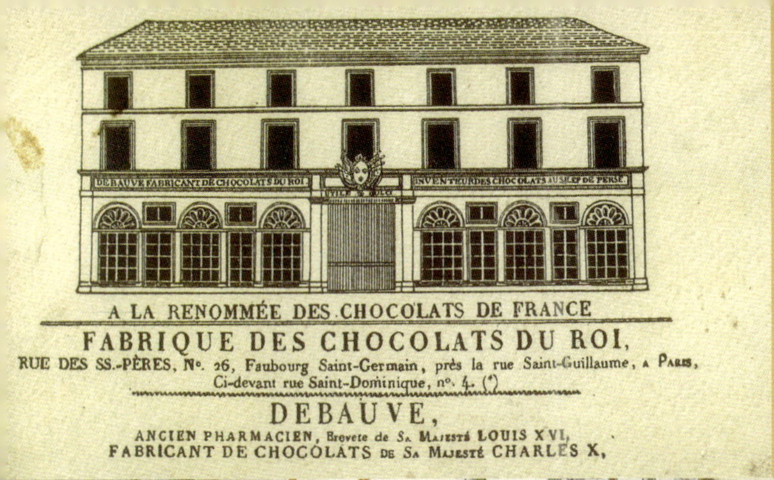

Advertisement of 1826, Debauve

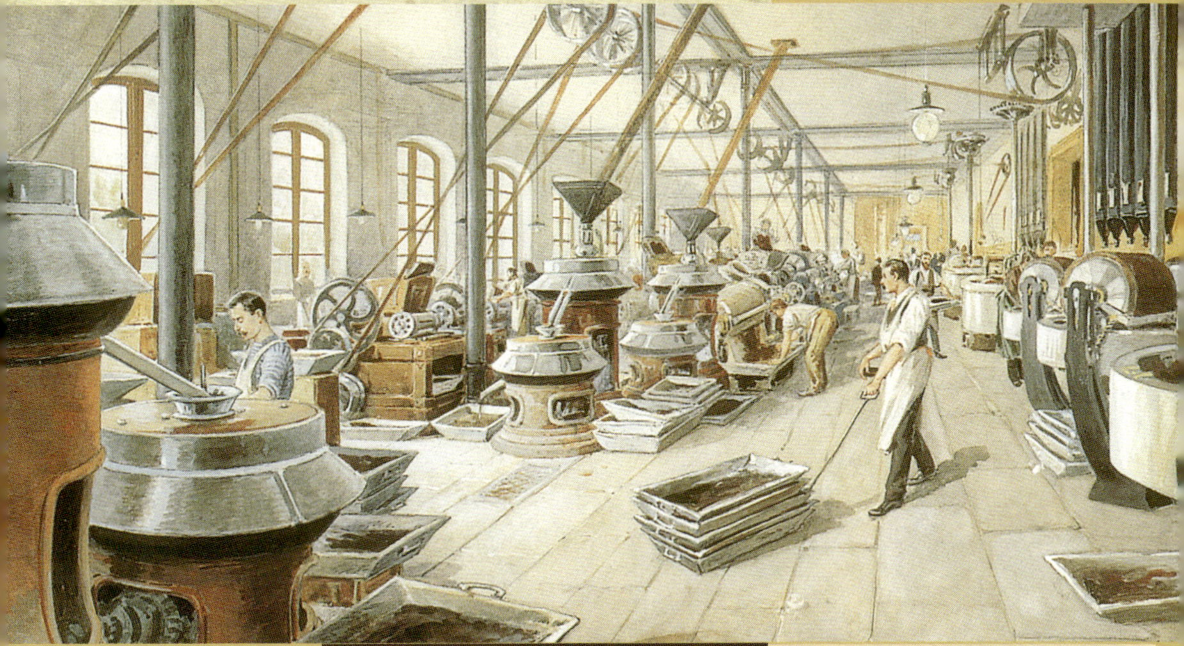

Grinding hall of a chocolate factory, end of the 20th century

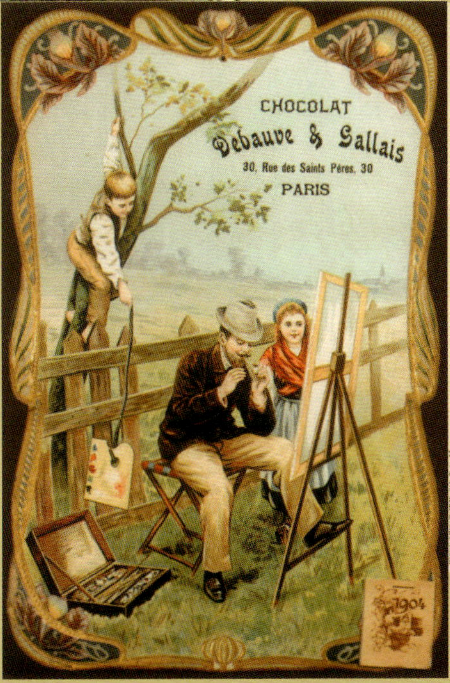

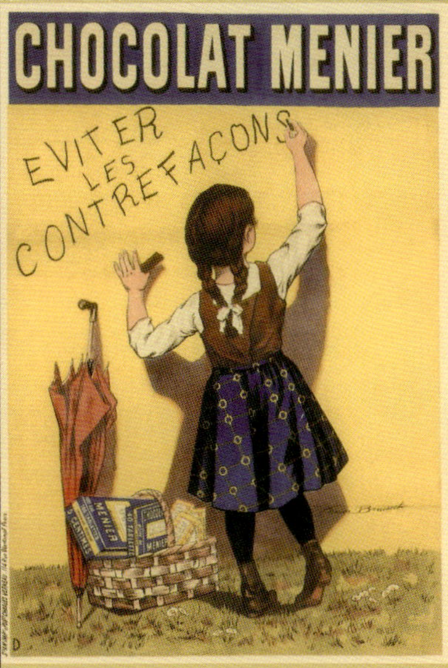

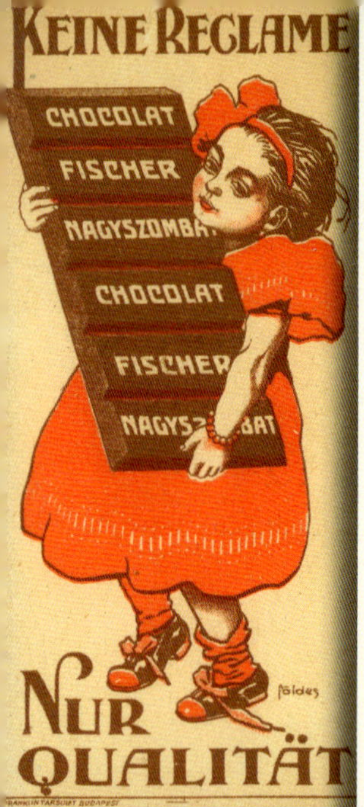

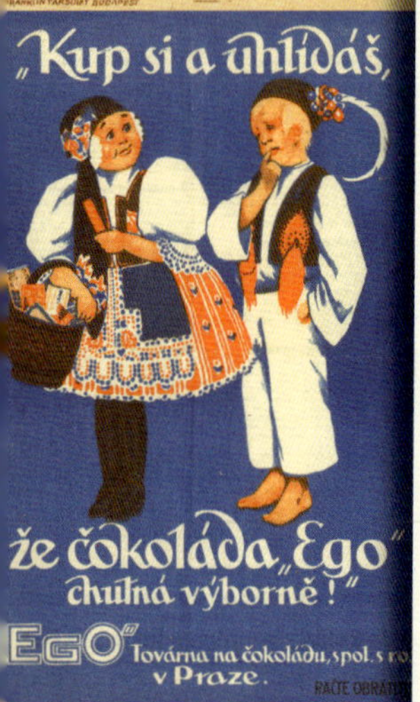

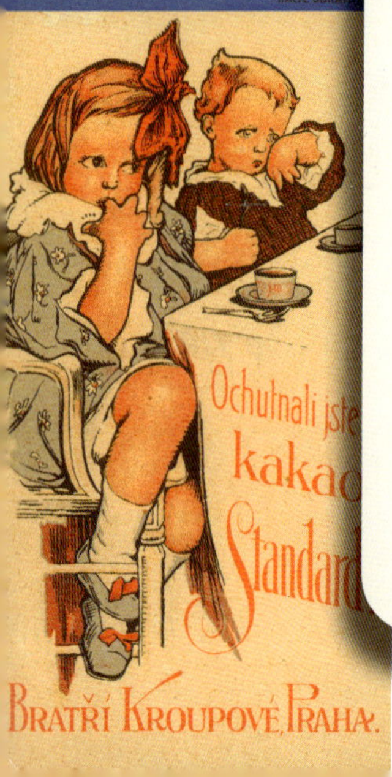

The history of the chocolate industry in the Czech Republic

Chocolate has been brought to the Czech Republic from Western European countries where drinking chocolate was very popular already in the 17th century. The first known chocolate trader was Filip Watzke living in the late 18th century in the house called Black Sun. This is an interesting fact, because the Choco-Story Museum was established in the next-door house.

The oldest producers

Luna Praha, established by Frantisek Černoch in Kozí Street in 1839, is supposed to be the oldest producer of chocolate.
Its first product has been called 'Chocolate with Indian'.
Deli Lovosice was established in 1806 by August Tschinkel for production of coffee imitation. They started to produce chocolate in 1858. Fiedor Opava (nowadays Opavia) was established in 1840, for the production of biscuits and later also chocolate.
Their well-known specialty Fidorka is popular even nowadays.

Period 1850-1900

Many companies were established in the second half of the 19th century, amongst which the most popular were:
Ph. Kneisl, renamed Sfinx Všetuly-Holešov in Moravia, founded in 1863. Their trade mark Sfinx is still on the market.
Velim ve Velimi was established by a Hungarian aristocrat in 1869.
A. Marsner, Praha-Vinohrady, started before 1890. Today is called Orion – best selling chocolate in the Czech Republic.
Zora Olomouc, established in 1898. Today the biggest Czech chocolate factory is owned by Nestlé.
Diana-Hartwig a Vogel, Podmokly - Děčín (est. in 1893).
Stolwerck Brothers Bratislava (est. in 1896) nowadays Figaro Bratislava, owned by Kraft Foods.

Period 1901-1920

In this period the following companies and many more started production:
Standard, Brothers Kroupa Praha-Vokovice, in 1903.
Kolinea Kolín, in 1906.
Fischer Trnava, Slovakia, in 1906, since 1934 the company uses the trade mark Figaro.

Koukol and Michera, Kutná Hora, established in 1912, with the well-known trade mark Lidka.
Rupa Praha, established in 1914 by Rudolf Pachl, nationalized after 1945, since 1996 the name is used again by a newly established company.

Period after 1920

There were over 100 factories in former Czechoslovakia between 1920-1940. Some of them were:
Bonbonia Bratři Makalové Kolín, established in 1920.
Maryša Hodonín, established in 1920.
Deva Trebišov, established in 1951, the only chocolate factory built during the communist era.

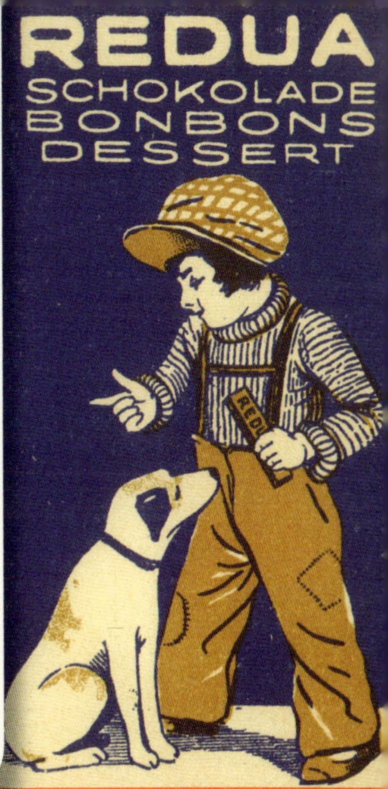

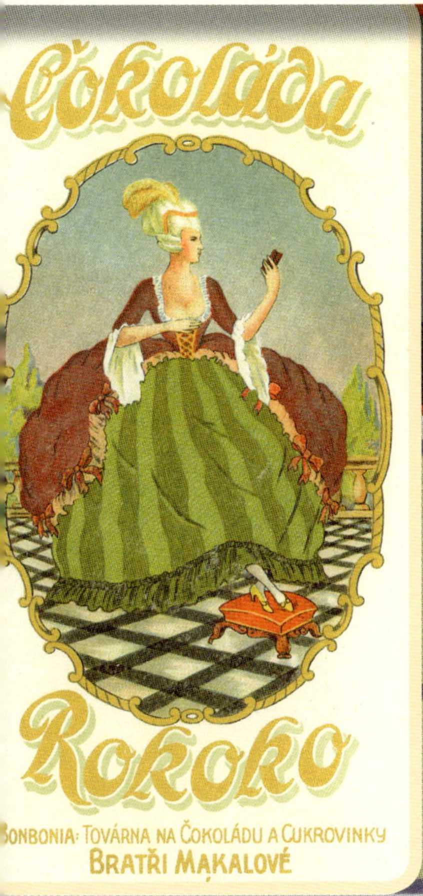

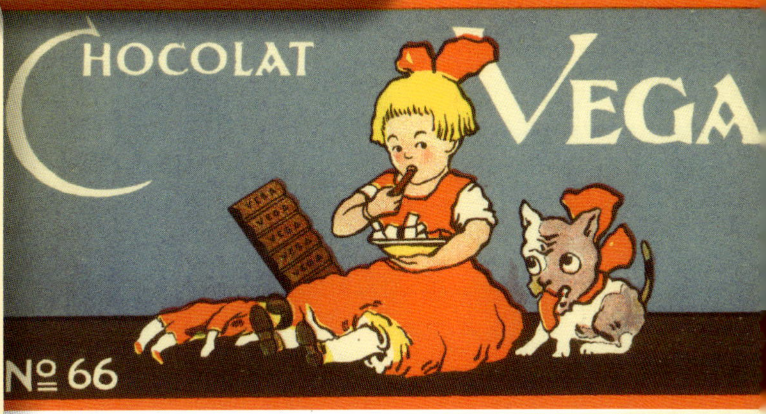

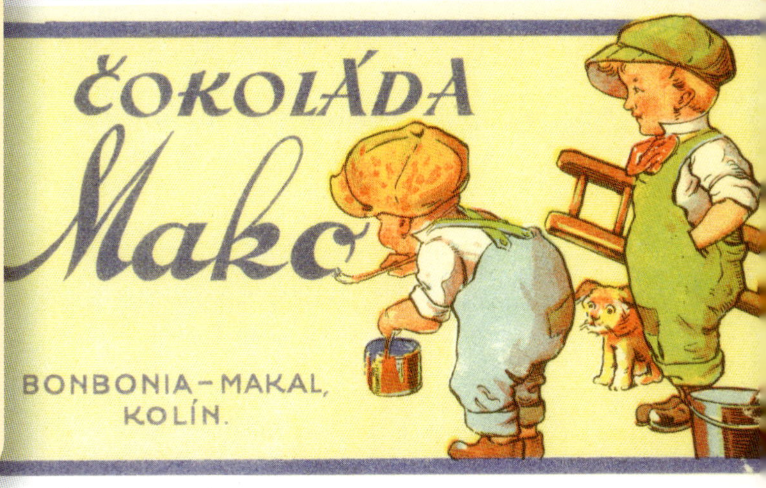

This information guide has been compiled by the Choco-Story museums especially for its visitors.

Choco-Story Brugge
Wijnzakstraat 2 (Sint Jansplein), B-8000 Brugge
Tel/Fax : +32 (0)50.61.22.37
e-mail : info@choco-story.be
www.choco-story.be

Choco-Story
Le musée gourmand du chocolat
28 Bd Bonne Nouvelle, F-75010 Paris
Tel : +33(0)1.42.29.68.60
Fax :+33(0)1.42.29.65.08
e-mail : info@museeduchocolat.fr
www.museeduchocolat.fr

Choco-Story Prague
Celetna 10, CZ-110 00 Praha 1
Tel : +420.224.242.953
e-mail : info@choco-story-praha.cz
www.choco-story-praha.cz

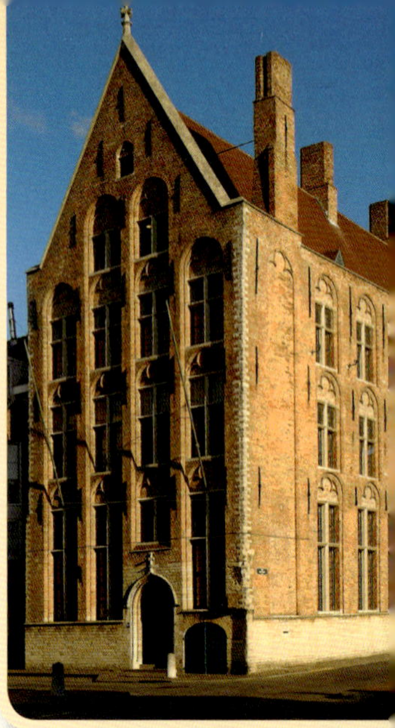

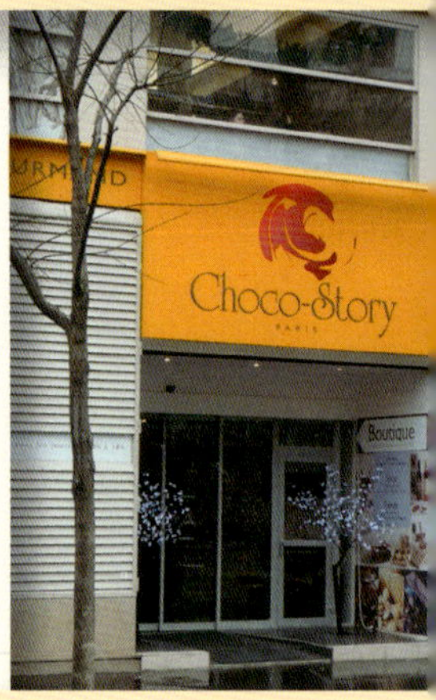

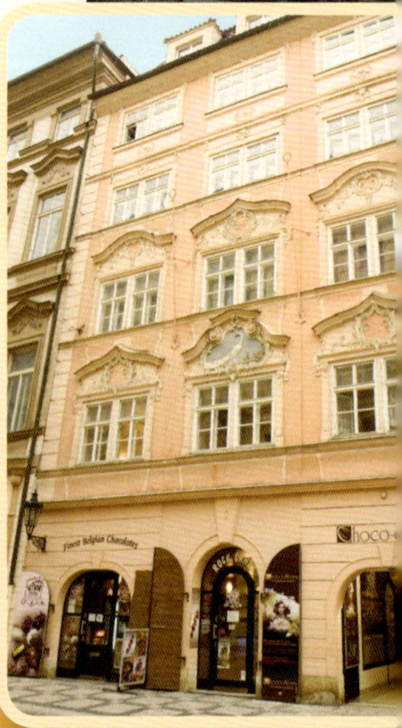

Lay-out: Jan de Coster
Printed by PurePrint, Oostkamp www.pureprint.be
An edition of Stichting Kunstboek www.stichtingkunstboek.com

ISBN 978-90-5856-370-5
D/2011/6407/7